ABRAHAM COWLEY

104200

A DISSERTATION

FOR

THE DEGREE OF DOCTOR IN PHILOSOPHY

IN

THE UNIVERSITY OF BERNE

BY

EMMA A. YARNALL.

Berne
Printed by Stæmpfli & Co.
1897.

ABRAHAM COWLEY.

The 17ᵗʰ Century.

Abraham Cowley was born in the early part of a Century which was to prove the most eventful in the history of the British Isles.

A Century which was to combat the "right divine of kings to govern wrong". A Century which was to see the life of a king taken by his subjects —not because he was a wicked ruler—an old story in the history of the world—not because he was a profligate as was Louis XV.; not because he was a tyrant in the manner of his ancestor, Henry the VIII.; but because the germs of self-government were stirring to life in the Anglo-Saxon race and a new order of things was to be introduced.

Heredity was no longer to be a reason why a people should be governed by the vacillating will of a weak ruler.

A Century of two Revolutions. The second necessary to complete what the first had begun. Abraham Cowley was born in 1618. In the second decade of this Century of Revolutions. A boundary period in Politics as in Literature. The reign of the Tudors— with its glory and its despotism—was past. In the future lowered the black clouds of the "Great Rebellion" which was to change the old order. The great and glorious Elizabethan period was in its autumn glories and a new order of things was here also about to be ushered in. Not with the drum beat and the horrors of civil war, but a change none the less real and vital for the history of Literature in England. Shakespeare, Beaumont—Spenser were gone —"Bare Ben" was still to be seen at the "Mermaid" surrounded by his few surviving friends. Bacon was living but shorn of his glory. Milton was ten years of age. Of Cowley's most famous friends, Davenant and Denham, were only three years older than he.

Waller was 13 years older. Dryden was born 13 years later.

The war of the "Roses" in the 15th Century is oft quoted as a reason for the dearth of Literature in that Century.

With the same reasoning and with the oft repeated "inter Arma silent Musæ" should we not expect a like result from the 17th Century? We shall find, however, this period so prolific in political changes and marked by a civil war, not a barren one in literature, though not boasting of the brilliant names which graced the preceding Elizabethan age, or the following Queen Anne period.

Sketch of the Poet's Life.

Cowley was born in London—in the centre of busy, bustling London. Not an ideal place for the birth of a poet, we should say; yet nature laughs at our reasoning and deposits one of her choice spirits in an Ayrshire hut and another in the centre of London.

Aubrey, Wood, Johnson and most of the other authorities have stated that Cowley was born "at London in Fleet Street near the end of Chancery Lane" and that his father was a grocer. It has been reserved for an American Genealogist, Colonel Chester, to show, with almost absolute certainty, that Cowley was the son of a stationer, Thomas Cowley, of the Parish of St. Michael le Querne, a church in Cheapside, which was destroyed by the "fire" and not rebuilt. The registers of this church were burnt but the will of the aforesaid Thomas Cowley has been found among the wills of the Prerogative Court of Canterbury. [1])

Peter Cunningham had already, in 1854, stated the same in his edition of Dr Johnson's "Lives of the Poets". [2]) Not having given his authority, no importance was attached to his statement.

Cowley's father died before his birth and his early years were guided by his mother.

As the father, according to his friend Sprat, left "sufficient estate" it is pleasant to know that our poet's early years were not oppressed by the "res angusta domi".

His days of adverse fortune come later in life. We can think of him, therefore, as a happy little boy enjoying life as only a boy can, emulating the words of Longfellow:

A boy's will is the wind's will
And the thoughts of youth are long, long thoughts.

His mother seems to have been equal to the task of caring for the mind as well as the body of her

[1]) See Grosart's Memorial Introduction to his "Complete Works of Cowley", p. 10, 1881.

[2]) 3 vols., 8°, 1854. — Vol. I, 3.

son. Through her efforts he was early sent to the Westminster school. She is represented as earnestly en-
deavoring to procure for her son the advantages of
a liberal education. She lived to the age of eighty
and therefore had her efforts rewarded by seeing
her son a great man. Sprat represents Cowley as
always a dutiful son, justly repaying her for her
tender care of his childhood.

Cowley had a gentle, amiable disposition which
won him many friends in Westminster school. The
little of his early history which we know he has told
us himself. Speaking of his love of the poets he says:[1]

> How this love came to be produced in me is a hard
> question. I believe I can tell the particular little chance that
> filled my head with such chimes of verse as have never since
> left ringing there, for I remember when I began to read and
> take some pleasure in it there was wont to lie in my mother's
> parlor (I know not by what accident, for she herself never
> read any book but of devotion), but there was wont to lie
> Spenser's Works; this I happened to fall upon and was in-
> finitely delighted with the stories of the Knights, and Giants,
> and Monsters and brave houses, which I found everywhere
> there, (tho' my understanding had little to do with all this),
> and by degrees with the tinkling of the rhyme and dance of
> the numbers, so that I think I had read him all over before
> I was twelve years old.

When we recall our experience with children
of ten and twelve we are fain to smile at Cowley's
modest recital. These lines are often quoted as a
proof that Cowley was *made* a poet by reading
Spenser. D[r] Johnson seems to have been of this
opinion as he says in this connection that a genius
is a mind of great natural power *accidentally* directed
into a particular channel. The "natural power" all

---

[1] "Cowley's Works", Edition of 1700, p. 131.

must agree to, but at the "*accidentally*" we think most would demur.

Some one has said: "Talent does what it *can,* Genius what it *must*."

We should rather say the poet soul leaped forth to greet the "Poet's poet" as a brother, and to revel in that which the great Macaulay called "a tedious poem". Cowley, while at Westminster school, showed wonderful precocity, perhaps the most wonderful on record. Milton, as well as Pope, may be said to have "lisped in numbers", but we have nothing from the former before his fifteenth year and from the latter before his fourteenth year. Even "the marvellous boy" Chatterton, was sixteen before he attracted the attention of the world. As is usual with highly gifted youths, the school curriculum was irksome, and we find that Cowley could never be induced to learn the rules of Grammar. We have a poem from him, however, "Pyramus and Thisbe", composed in his tenth year, and another "Constantia and Phile-tus" at twelve, which seldom violate the rules of Murray.

An Epic was also written, as we shall see, during his College Days. At the age of fifteen his first volume appeared: "Poetical Blossoms" by A. C.

This little book of 1633 is a quarto of thirty-two leaves. It is now very rare and one of the prizes of book collectors. A few months earlier appeared Milton's first printed *English* verses—the lines on Shakespeare prefixed to the second folio edition of 1632.

At the age of 18 Cowley entered Cambridge University where he remained seven years. For some unknown reason he had failed to be elected to a scholarship on the Westminster Foundation. His renown, however, procured him an open scholarship. He must have had a patron as Mrs. Cowley's means were not sufficient to equip her son for the University. It has been supposed Sir Kenelm Digby was this patron. Aubrey says he was "ever very kind" to Cowley. Nothing certain however is known in regard to it.

Cowley won at Cambridge the degree of Master of Arts in 1642, after having been in 1639 created an A. B.

The political troubles caused his expulsion from College together with his friend Crashaw, for refusing to take the oath at that time prescribed to all members of Cambridge University. He left Cambridge with a sorrowful heart as his Latin elegy addressed to the University testifies. We here quote some passages from it, translated by the Rev. Richard Wilton, M. A.

> Mother most rich from thy poor son to thee
> This scanty pledge of vast affection see.
> Ah, better gifts for thee I fain would pour
> Had but my grateful hands a larger store.
>
> *   *   *
>
> O name of Cambridge, o most pleasant sound!
> Deep in my heart the love of thee is found.
> Fair, without luxury, thy Halls are seen;
> And happy are the lives led there, I ween.
>
> *   *   *
>
> O Cam, Apollo thee most pleasant deems
> Tho' poor, yet envied by goldbearing streams!
> Ah, if God would your dear delights restore
> The learned leisure on your happy shore.
>
> *   *   *

Sprat in his usual guarded manner, says: "When the civil war broke out his affection to the Kings cause drew him to Oxford, as soon as it began to be the seat of the Royal party."

At St. John's College Oxford, he remained two years and there made many friends, among whom was Lord Falkland, one of the Principal Secretaries of State. Cowley became a partisan of the Royal party as was to be expected from one of his education and temperament. Sir John Elyot gives us a picture of Oxford at that time, of which Grosart says: [1])

It is a pitiable spectacle that is presented, much as if one were shown sane men and women adjusting their perukes and patches respectively, while an earthquake was shaking the solid earth beneath them, or a tempest crashing above them.

The war which had been threatening, now breaking over their heads Cowley, crossed with the Queen and her train, to France. Here he acted as secretary to the Queen and Lord Jermyn for 12 years. His employment was in deciphering the letters which passed between the King and Queen. He was also sent to Jersey, Scotland, Flanders and Holland on state business. His letters written in the interest of the Royalists, Grosart publishes for the first time from: "Miscellanea Aulica".[2])

These letters are of little interest to the general reader. One of them is quoted, with D[r] Johnson's remarks, farther on in these pages.

When the court of the Queen was broken up in Paris, Cowley was sent to England (1656) that he might, under the pretence of privacy and retirement, give notice of what was passing in England. He was

---

[1]) Grosart's Mem. Introduction, p. 20.
[2]) See Grosart's Cowley's Works, vol. II, pp. 343—353.

arrested, though in mistake for another person, and only set at liberty on a bail of £ 1000. On the death of Cromwell he crossed again to France where he remained till the Restoration.

This part of Cowley's life has been the subject of much criticism and much difference of opinion. His friend Sprat in his carefully written and guarded utterances—written while the civil war was recent and party spirit still rife (1668)—justifies his conduct and only seems anxious to give proofs of Cowley's loyalty. He says it was [1]) Cowley's opinion that a mistaken zeal for the King's cause hurried many of his followers to their ruin and that for himself he found it impossible to pursue the ends for which he came over if he did not make some kind of declaration of his peaccable intentions. In the preface to the edition of poems which Cowley published immediately on coming back to England, in 1656, he says he accepts [2]) the inevitable and treats the controversy as at an end as God seems to have decided against the Stuarts.

This compliance with the men in power was enough to make him unpopular with the Royal party. Some of the critics, however, seem to think there was no cause for the indifference with which he was treated by the King after the Restoration. "Mr Cowley's pardon is his reward", king Charles is quoted as having said when asked to reward Cowley for his loyalty.

Masson in his "Life of Milton" says, he thinks it was not possible for Cowley to live in London as a spy for the King's party as

---

[1]) Edition of 1784, p. 12.
[2]) Farther on in these pages see a portion of this Preface which was suppressed on its 1st publication. First published by Grosart.

· such a game could [1]) not have been played under the wachful eye of Thurloe.

He thinks it more than likely that Cowley was tired of exile and of a court with which he could have no real sympathy. Dr Johnson looked rather leniently on Cowley's compliance:

He promised little and that little justifiable [2]). It does not appear to have gained him confidence enough to be trusted without security, for the bond of his bail was never cancelled; nor that it made him think himself secure, for at the dissolution of Government, which followed the death of Oliver, he returned into France." Wood in his annals says [3]): by complying with the men in power (which was much taken notice of by the Royal party) he obtained an order to be created D^r of Physic which being done to his mind (whereby he gained the ill will of some of his friends) he went into France again, having made a copy of verses on Oliver's death.

Nothing more is known of these verses on Oliver's death to which Wood refers. The lines inserted in "Discourse by way of Vision concerning Cromwell" it is generally supposed, are the lines referred to. The degree of D^r of Physic Cowley received in 1657 in Oxford. There is no reason to believe he ever attempted to practise. Considering Botany as necessary to a physician he retired into the country, to Kent, to gather plants. It is not surprising that Botany in the mind of a poet should turn into poetry. The result was the six books on plants in Latin. In the first and second book he displays the qualities of herbs in elegiac verse.

In the 3rd and 4th he describes the beauty of flowers in different measures. In the 5th book he

---

[1]) Masson's Life of Milton, vol. 5, p. 83.

[2]) Johnson's Life of Cowley. Edition of 1783, p. 14.

[3]) From Johnson's Life of Cowley, p. 13.

describes a competition between the trees of America and those of the old world.

Pomona seated in one of the fortunate Isles between the two worlds, a convention of each is assembled before her. A quarrel between the trees of the old and the new world—naturally—ends the contest. The 6th book is wholly devoted to the honor of his country. He makes the British oak to preside in the assembly of forest trees, then enlarges upon the history of the "late troubles", the Kings afflictions and return, and the beginning of the Dutch war. These poems may be called—for the most part at least—a medical treatise on plants.

The physician is more prominent than the poet. The poems have not added to Cowley's reputation. They were translated by Nahum Tate and M[rs] Aphra Behn. The latter an admirer and an imitator of Cowley.

The biographer of the great Lord Fairfax [1]), Clements R. Markham, gives us the following glimpse of Cowley's social life:

A gay and brilliant wedding at Bolton Percy church on Sept. 14th 1657, attended by all the families of the neighborhood and Cowley, the Dukes best man, wrote the following sonnet in honor of the occasion:

Now blessing to thy noble choice betide,
Happy and happy—making bride!
Tho' thou art of a victorious race,
And all their rougher victory dost grace
With gentle triumphs of thy face,
Permit us in this nobler war to prize
No less thy yielding heart than thy victorious eyes.
Nor doubt the honor of that field
Where thou didst first o'ercome ere thou didst yield,
And tho' thy Father's martial name

---

[1]) Grosart's Mem. Introd., p. 24.

Has filled the trumpets and the drums of fame,
Thy husband triumphs now no less than he,
And it may justly questioned be
Which was the happiest conqueror of the three.

This was the marriage of George Villiers, Duke of Buckingham, with Mary Fairfax, who had Andrew Marvell for a Tutor, in whose lovely garden poems she has been immortalized, and who is styled *"Princess"* on her tomb in Henry VII's chapel. Well for the happy "Princess" that the dark clouds of coming events "cast no shadows before".

Cowley was gone before his friend and patron, but Mary, the bride, outlived the troublous times and died in 1704.

Cowley had been promised the Mastership of Savoy, but his petition for the long-promised boon was refused. Caused by some "enemy of the Muses" is Word's opinion.

Cowley expressed his discontent in a poem called the "Complaint" in which he describes himself as the "Melancholy Cowley" lying under the black shade of the "Yew's unlucky green", where reverend Cam cuts out his famous way. It was well ridiculed by suckling in the following lines:

Savoy—Missing Cowley came into the court
Making apologies for his bad play:
Every one gave him so good a report,
That Apollo gave heed to all he could say;
Nor would he have had, 'tis thought, a rebuke,
Unless he had done some notable folly,
Write verses unjustly in praise of Sam Tuke,
Or, printed his pitiful melancholy.

Cowley's supplanter in the Mastership of Savoy was one of the Killigrews, brother of the notarious Tom Killigrew, groom of the bed-chamber to Charles II.

One would naturally expect that if anyone deserved a reward—that one was Cowley, who had given the best years of his young life to the despairing cause of the king.

Cowley was not the man to make himself a favorite in the Court of Charles II.

His rigid and even "austere life" and love of learning made him the object of distrust and suspicion in the gay circle which surrounded the King.

Cowley, in his despair thought of going to America but his fortune was at too low an ebb—he had not sufficient to defray the expense of the voyage. His friends Lord St. Alban and the Duke of Buckingham made provision for him. Being weary of active life and longing for the retirement which the cruel war had denied to him, he resolved to retire into the country and there pass the remainder of his life. His desire for solitude and retirement from the world, has been much sneered at as insincere. Dr Johnson, to whom a walk down Fleet Street touching each lamp-post as he passed, was the acme of human bliss and who could not appreciate the desire expressed by Cowley, sneeringly recommends these who „pant for solitude" to read Cowley's letter to Sprat describing his coming to Chertsey.

Here we must disagree with the great "master of the art of putting down".

No one, open to conviction, can doubt from the essays of Cowley, written in his retirement, as well as from passages scattered through his writings, that he had the genuine love for country life, which so often accompanies the gift of genius. Of the letter in question Stebbing says:

Surely the catalogue of ills in this epistle was compiled in sport and by a very cheerful mind.

The following amusing epitaph composed by Cowley, in Latin, and supposed to be written on his house in the country, certainly shows him in a "merry mood".

Epitaphium Vivi Authoris.

Hic, o viator, sub Lare parvulo
Couleius hic est conditus, hic jacet
Defunctus humani laboris
Sorte, supervacuaque vita.

Non indecora pauperie nitens,
Et non inerti nobilis otio,
Vanoque dilectis popello
Divitiis animosus hostis.

Possis ut illum dicere mortuum,
En Terra jam nunc quantula sufficit?
Exempta sit curis, Viator,
Terra sit illa levis, precare.

Hic sparge flores, sparge breves rosas,
Nam vita gaudet mortua floribus,
Herbisque odoratis corona
Vatis adhuc cinerem calentem.

The following translation is from the pen of William Cullen Bryant who ignorant of other translations thus introduces his: "The task of translating such lines is not easy, but here is an attempt to put the thought into English verse:

The Living Author's Epitaph.

Here, stranger, in this lowly spot,
The buried Cowley finds at last,
Rest from the labors of his lot,
And leaves life's follies with the past.

In not unseemly low estate,
Nor meanly slothful, tho' retired,
Well hath the poet learned to hate
The wealth by staring crowds admired.

Yea, speak of him as dead; for see
How little earth is now his share;
And, stranger, pray that light may be
Its burden, and may bring no care.

Strew flowers; they please the living dead ;
Here roses ere they wither strew,
And o'er his yet warm ashes shed
The sweetest smelling herbs that grow.

Cowley himself says "I thought when I went first to dwell in the country that, without doubt, I should have met there with the simplicity of the old poetical age; I thought to have found no inhabitants there but such as the shepherds of Sir Philip Sidney in Arcadia, or of monsieur d'Urfe upon the banks of Lignon; and began to consider with myself which way I might recommend the happiness and innocence of the men of Chertsey ; but to confess the truth, I perceived quickly, by infallible demonstrations, that I was still in old England, and not in Arcadia or La Forrest".

The rest and silence of the grave Cowley did not have as the frequent visits of his friends testify. The most authentic sources of evidence in regard to this subject are Sprat's life of Cowley and the diaries of Pepys and Evelyn. Pepys speaks of his fame as preeminent and refers to his life with respect but nothing like pity. Evelyn says the retirement suited his mind better than his body and adds that Cowley had numerous invitations to return to active life but he never gave ear to any persuasions of profit or of preferment.

The foundation of the opinion that he was sad and morose in his retirement rests principally on the "Complaint" and that was written to reproach the court for failure to reward his long years of fidelity. Wood's assertion that he was a "gloomy man" in his retirement is unsupported by the testimony of his intimate friends.

Cowley did not live long to enjoy the pleasures of a country life. He died at the Porch House, Chertsey, in 1667, July 28th.

The court paid him funeral honors. The Duke of Buckingham reared his monument in "Poet's Corner" beside the ashes of Chaucer and Spenser. Denham wrote his elegy and Sprat is said to have written the following epitaph, the original being in Latin:

Here lies the Pindar, Horace, and Virgil
of the English nation.[1])

While thro' the world thy labors shine
Bright as thyself thou bard divine;
Thou in thy fame wilt live and be
A partner with eternity.

Here in soft peace forever rest,
Soft as the love that filled thy breast;
Let hoary faith around thy urn,
And all the watchful muses mourn.

Forever sacred be this room,
May no rude hand disturb thy tomb;
Or sacrilegious rage or lust
Affront thy venerable dust.

Sweet Cowley's dust let none profane;
Here may it undisturbed remain;
Eternity not take but give,
And make this stone forever live.

Nobles attended his funeral and followed his bier on its passage down the Thames to the Abbey.

Tears the river shed
When the sad pomp along its banks
Was led.

---

[1]) Cowley's Works. Edition of 1784, 4th vol.

King Charles on hearing of his death said:
"Mr. Cowley has not left a better man behind him
in England."

John Evelyn who was present at the funeral
gives the following lines in his diary:

3rd August 1667.

Went to Cowley's funerall, whose corps lay at Walling-
ford House (Duke of Buckingham's) and was thence conveyed
to Westminster Abbey in a hearse with 6 horses and all funerall decency, neere one hundred coaches of noblemen and
persons of qualitie following; among these all the witts of the
towne, divers Bishops and Clergymen. He was interred next
Geoffrey Chancer and neere Spenser. A goodly monument is
since erected to his memorie.[1]

Porch House, Guilford Street, is still shown with a
verse from Pope's "Windsor Forest", slightly modified, over the door.

Here the last accents flowed from Cowley's tongue.

The House, in Cowley's time, stood within the
Town, but surrounded by ample gardens and skirted
by a brook, with St. Anne's steep declivities rising
at a little distance.

This place was the third which Cowley tried as
a place of residence after he left London. Battersea,
he first tried, but finding it unhealthy, he removed
to Barn Elms. Beneath the Elms which gave the
place its name, was a fashionable promenade where
Pepys "loved to display his newest and gayest
plumage". Here Cowley must have had more of the
"Vanity Fair" than he wished.

Cowley's Will[2]) was signed and sealed on
Sept. 28th, 1665. He leaves the most of his posses-.
sions to his brother Thomas. To Davenant £ 20.

---

[1]) "Evelyn's Diary" II. 222, Bicker's edition.
[2]) See Grosart's Mem. Introd., p. 28.

To Sprat £ 20. To the poor of the town of Chertsey
£ 20. To Sprat he left his study, books, and the re-
vision of all his writings with the request to let
nothing pass to the public which would give offence
to religion or morals.

Sprat's Life of Cowley.

Sprat's Life of Cowley is the only one written
by a contemporary. The work is called by Gosse
"an admirable piece of stately Biography" and by
Dʳ Johnson characterized as "a funeral oration rather
than a history". We naturally expect much from a
contemporary, but biography was a branch of literature late to blossom in England, and nothing of the
genus Boswell meets us here. We hear much panegyric, high praises of his character and writings,
but scarcely feel as though we stand face to face with
our poet—do not feel intimately acquainted with him
as we do with the great Samuel after reading Boswell's immortal work.

Still the words of Sprat will ever have a deep
interest for all admirers of Cowley as coming from
his intimate friend. Cowley's character is thus described by him:

He had a perfect natural goodness which neither the
uncertainties of his condition, nor the largeness of his wit
could pervert. He had a firmness and strength of mind that
was proof against the art of Poetry itself. Nothing vain or
fantastical, nothing flattering or insolent appeared in his
humor.

He had a great integrity and plainness of manners which
he preserved to the last, tho' much of his time was spent in
a nation and way of life that is not famous for sincerity.
But the truth of his heart was above the corruptions of all
examples.

There was nothing affected or singular in his habit, or person, or gesture. He understood the forms of good breeding enough to practise them without burdening himself or others. His modesty and humility were so great that if he had not had many other equal virtues, they might have been thought dissimulation.

His conversation was certainly of the most excellent kind; for, it was such as was rather admired by his familiar friends than by strangers at first sight. He surprised no man at first with any extraordinary appearance; he never thrust himself violently into the good opinion of his company. He was content to be known by leisure and by degrees, and so the esteem that was conceived of him, was better grounded and more lasting. None but his intimate friends ever discovered him a great poet by his discourse.

He was a passionate lover of liberty and freedom from constraint both in actions and in words.

His friendships were inviolable. The same men with whom he was familiar in his youth were his nearest acquaintance at the day of his death.

Sprat was an imitator of Cowley, writing Odes of a very "distressing nature". He was interested in science. In 1667 appeared his "History of the Royal Society", which had then been only five years in existence. It was founded on the 15th of July, 1662. "One of the few creditable occurrences in the reign of Charles II", says Masson.[1]

. Cowley was one of the first Fellows of the Royal Society. One of his finest poems is addressed to this Society. It contains the oft quoted lines:[2]

> Bacon, like Moses, led us forth at last,
> The barren wilderness he passed,
> Did on the very border stand
> Of the blest promised land,
> And from the mountain's top of his exalted wit
> Saw it himself and showed us it.

---

[1] Masson's Life of Milton, vol. 6, p. 395.
[2] Cowley's Works, 1700, p. 35.

But life did never to one man allow
Time to discover worlds and conquer too;
Nor can so short a line sufficient be
To fathom the vast depths of nature's sea.

Some one has said that this poem was nothing less than the first book of the "Novum Organum", transfigured into poetry. In his lines to Dᵣ Charleton Dryden expresses the same thought in regard to Bacon:

The longest tyranny that ever swayed,
Was that wherein our ancestors betrayed
Their freeborn reason to the Stagirite,
And made his torch their universal light.
So truth, while only one supplied the state,
Grew scarce and dear and yet sophisticate;
Still it was taught like emp'ric wares or charms,
Hard words, sealed up with Aristotle's arms.

Johnson's Life of Cowley.

In Dᵣ Johnson's "Lives of the poets" Cowley stands first. He is there classed with the poets whom the critic is pleased to call "Metaphysical", and much space is taken up with examples to show us why he has so called them, and with examples from Cowley to prove that he also belongs to that group. This epithet began and ended with Dᵣ Johnson, we believe, but at the time was quite popular. Johnson gives Donne as the founder of this style in England.

Dryden in his dedication to Juvenal 1693 says: Doune affects the Metaphysics not only in his satires, but in his amorous verses where nature only should reign. Southey says of this designation:[1]

It is not fortunate, but so much respect is due to Johnson that it would be unbecoming to substitute, even if it were easy to propose, one which might be unexceptionable.

---

[1] Southey's Life of Cowper, II, p. 127.

Cowley was undoubtedly influenced by Donne as well as the then prevailing taste to adopt this style.

Gosse says of Donne: [1])

That extraordinary writer cast his shadow over the vault of the Century from its beginning to its close, like one of those Carthaginian statues, the hands and feet of which supported opposite extremities of the arch they occupied.

Southey says in one of his essays:

The metaphysical school which marred a good poet in Cowley, and found its proper direction in Butler, expired in Norris of Bemerton.

Dr Johnson says of these poets: [2])

They were men of learning and to show their learning was their chief endeavor; but unluckily resolving to show it in rhyme, instead of writing poetry, they only wrote verses, and very often such verses as stood the trial of the finger better than the ear; for the modulation was so imperfect, that they were found to be verses only by counting the syllables. If poetry be an imitative art, these writers lose their right to the name of poet, for they cannot be said to have imitated anything; they neither copied nature nor life; neither painted the forms of matter nor represented the operations of intellect. The most heterogeneous ideas are yoked by violence together; nature and art are ransacked for illustrations, comparisons and allusions.

To many of these faults Cowley must certainly plead guilty, but the criticisms of the great Doctor must be taken with limitations—"whatever may be conceded to Johnson as a moralist and lexicographer, poetical criticism was not his province". The declining euphuism of the 17th Century cannot be defended or admired by a 19th Century reader, yet

[1]) Preface to "17th Century Studies", 1885, p. 9.
[2]) Johnson's Life of Cowley, p. 25.

many a noble thought and many a true gem of poetry may be found in the works of these old writers.

In regard to D[r] Johnson's Life of Cowley Mr. Humphrey Ward has said: "It has eclipsed for almost every one the works of its author." [1])

No true lover of Cowley can echo this opinion. Grosart's criticism is in our opinion more just. Of the Life he says:

Its *criticism* has been its preserving salt. As a life, in common with most of the Lives, it is inaccurate as well as meagre, and the facts so given as rather to furnish pegs upon which to hang grandiose dissertation or texts from which to preach sonorous platitudes, seasoned with spite, than to tell the life-story.

Matthew Arnold does not include the life of Cowley in his specimens of D[r] Johnson's finest work.

Gosse.

Professor Edmund Gosse in his 17th Century Studies, 1885, gives us a delightful paper on Cowley. While considering Mr. Gosse one of our most agreable and genial writers and critics, and we may also add—lecturers—as the writer has had the good fortune to sit under a course of lectures from Prof. Gosse—we must still entirely disagree with him in regard to Cowley's fame. It comes with a strange sound to our ears and is read with sad astonishment that Cowley's fame as a poet is "a dead name or only living in depreciation and ridicule"—sad indeed if these words are true of *Old* England.

These lines were written before the delightful work of Grosart came to hand. The writer learns

---

[1]) The English Poets, 1880, vol. II, p. 235.

with delight that Cowley has a true friend and
admirer in his native land, who is so competent to
defend his fame and place him where he so well
deserves to stand among England's "Worthies".

Grosart bombards most unrelentingly the Hallams,
Wards and Gosses who have presumed to rob Cowley
of his well earned and enduring fame. Among the
many letters of thanks and sympathy which he received, came one which had been tossed on the waves of
the broad Atlantic—from our ever revered William
Cullen Bryant. This voice from "New England's
rocky strand", and now alas, from the *"Jenseits"*
in a wider sense, comes as a gladly welcomed con-
firmation and support of the above expressed opinion.

Professor Gosse has made a noble effort—if
wholly unnecessary—to rescue Cowley from the
supposed oblivion into which he has fallen. His essay
will be read with pleasure by true lovers of our
literature as well as by every admirer of Cowley's
writings.

Stebbing.

In his interesting Essay, one of the best modern
contributions to our literary history, Stebbing calls
Cowley "The Poet Politician". Cowley was surely
never in any true sense of the word a *politician.*
In such a contest as was then raging, neutrality
was impossible. That a youthful poet as Cowley
should serve the Queen was natural and to be expected, and more especially as circumstances threw
him under her personal influence. That a youth
whose tastes and education were not such as to
enable him to grasp fully the tremendous issues at
stake, should take sides with the King of the "narrow
forehead and melancholy Vandyke air", who was

admired and beloved by those who came within the immediate sphere of his influence—is certainly not a sufficient reason for naming him a politician. Grosart has given the following opinion:[1])

I cannot think it is doing injustice to Cowley to adjudge the sincerity of his loyalty to a personal sentiment rather than to principle and conscience. His *heart,* not his *head* ruled and overruled him.

Had Cowley been a politician his play, one thinks, would have shown more tact—more capacity for grasping the situation and would have been better adapted to please the fickle crowd of court favorites and followers. What politician could have made the reference to Virgil in the following lines which are taken from a letter on the subject of the Scotch treaty:[2])

The Scotch treaty is the only thing now in which we are vitally concerned; I am one of the last hopers and yet cannot now abstain from believing that an agreement will be made; all people upon the place incline to that of Union— and to tell the truth (which I take to be an agreement above all the rest) Virgil has told the same thing to that purpose.

Dr Johnson thinks the times were so tinged with superstition that Cowley may have consulted the Virgilian *lots* and have had an answer from the oracle to which he trusted. Cowley's easy acquiescence in what he called *"the inevitable"* and his apparent submission to Cromwell savor little of the true politician. The 17th Century and a residence in London during the civil war would have developed the latent powers of a born politician..

It is as difficult to think of the poet Cowley as a politician as to imagine a " mute inglorious

---

[1]) Memorial Introd., p. 17.
[2]) Johnson's Life of Cowley, p. 10.

Milton". In his retirement, says Stebbing, Cowley laid aside the politician. The garment was an easy one to throw aside as it had never sat easily upon the wearer. Cowley hated despotism, but he had not the inclination, perhaps not the ability to grasp the salient points in the conflict, and as the many, under such circumstances, dreaded a revolution. Being more willing to bear the ills he had than to "fly to others that he knew not of". In Cowley's youth, at Westminster school, he was under an influence which if continued might have made him a follower of Milton and Marvell. Lambert Osbalston, head-master of Westminster, to whom Cowley dedicated his "Pyramus and Thisbe", was an adherent of the popular party. It is interesting to imagine what change might have been wrought in Cowley through contact with Milton and Marvell instead of Jermyn and Buckingham. Cowley could, as Stebbing remarks, "praise excellent Brutus and flatter and cooperate with mean-spirited Jermyn" without apparently any consciousness of inconsistency. This can easily be explained. It was the accident of birth and association which made Cowley a supporter of Monarchy. No one can study his life without feeling he had the true spirit of a Brutus. A Brutus in the freer atmosphere of the 17th Century. Under a Monarch who, with all his faults, had so much of the "sweetness and light" in his personality, that we must ever uncover our heads with awe before the terrible majesty of the "people's voice" which could quietly and calmly, guided by the star of liberty alone, condemn such a monarch to the scaffold.

Cowley, though not made of martyr stuff, had many noble traits which stand out in bold relief against the dark and gloomy background of an age

which truly "tried men's souls". If we compare
him, for example, to Waller, how great the contrast.
How beautifull his fidelity to his friend Crashaw and
to a court with which he had no thought in common
Had he chosen to sue for favor and pardon, he
might, in the general scramble for preferment, which
followed the Restoration, have secured for himself
a lucrative position. On the side of the Royalists
there is no character which stands so easiliy, head
and shoulders, above contemporaries as that of our
poet. To quote Grosart: [1])

Pure among the vile, patriotic among the merely courtly,
noble among the venal, simple in his habits and likings among
the spendthrift and foully gay, and a fine old English gentleman.

And from Bryant:

Whatever may be the merit of any of his different
poems, the reader finds in none of them any stain of that
grossness which in the latter part of Cowley's life after
Charles II. brought his ribald court into England, had become
fashionable. Everything which he wrote has a certain expression of the purity of his own character.

Addison thus writes of him in his account of
the English Poets.

Blest man: whose spotless life and charming lays
Employed the tuneful prelate in his praise,
Blest man! who now shall be forever known
In Sprat's successful labors and thy own.

The letters of Cowley which Sprat and Clifford
felt justified in not giving to the world, would undoubtedly have been valuable aids in forming a just
estimate of his character.

Mary Russell Mitford closes her essay on Cowley
with what Grosart calls "uncharacteristic vehemence"
thus:

---

[1]) Memorial Introd., p. 22.

I cannot conclude without a word of detestation towards Sprat, who, Goth and Vandal that he was, destroyed the familiar letters of Cowley.

It is by no means certain that the letters were really distroyed by Sprat, and there is a bare possibility that they may yet be brought to light. Such an indefatigable researcher as Grosart, however, has failed to trace them.

Grosart.

Cowley has waited long, to the declining 19th Century, for an editor who would do him full justice.

Grosart's "Complete Works of Abraham Cowley in Verse and Prose", in two 4to volumes, appeared in 1881. Published by private subcription, forming one of the "Chertsey Worthies' Library".

The official letters, the suppressed part of the 1656 preface, "The Guardian" and the later "Cutter of Coleman Street", the two youthful dramas, all are for the first time given together in a convenient form. "The Memorial Introduction" leaves nothing to be desired in regard to the literature concerning Cowley, and his most enthusiastic admirers cannot ask a better ehampion than Grosart. Our frequent references to this noble work may give some idea of its value to those to whom it is not accessible. The second Cowley desideratum was supplied in 1887 by the neat little volume of "Cowley's Prose Works", by Rev. J. Rawson Lumby.

Pyramus and Thisbe.

The first production of Cowley, the poem of "Pyramus and Thisbe" was a wonderful production for a boy of ten. In it he was bold enough—the fearlessness of youth—to attempt a new stanza. Six lines rhyming a, b, a, a, b, b. The plot is the old story introduced by Shakespeare in "Midsummer Night's Dream".

It is not difficult to discover that Cowley had read Shakespeare as well as Spenser. It is written in the heroic verse and wonderfully well conducted. Some of the stanzas might well be envied by adult poets. Cowley afterwards (1636—56) improved his youthful poems, but as Grosart remarks—"what we want to-day is the boy-poets workmanship, not the man's". Sprat in his edition printed the revised text and was followed by others. Grosart gives the original text from the early volumes, as well as the so called later improvements. The following verses are taken from Grosart's edition:

4th stanza.

Like as a bird which in a net is taine,
By struggling more entangles in the ginne,
So they who in love's Labirinth remaine,
With striuing never can a freedom gaine;
The way to enter 's broad; but being in,
No art, no labour can an exit win.

*   *   *

Thus beauty is by beauties means undone,
Striuing to close those eyes that make her bright.

Thisbe's Song.

Come love, why stay'st thou? The night
Will vanish ere wee taste delight.
The moone obscures her selfe from sight,
Thou absent, whose eyes give her light.

Come quickly deare, be briefe as time,
Or we by morne shall be o'retane,
Love's Joy's thine owne as well as mine,
Spend not therefore, time in vaine.

Epitaph.

Underneath this marble stone,
Lie two beauties joyn'd in one.

Two whose loves, death could not sever,
For both liv'd, both dy'd together.

Two whose soules, being too divine
For earth, in their own spheare now shine,

Who have left their loves to Fame,
And their earth to earth againe.

His next performance, in his twelfth year, was
"Constantia and Philetus". The promise of the first
work, as is often the case, was not fully realized by
the second. In many respects, though more correct, it
is not equal to the first It is rather singular that
the child should be so much the father of the man [1]),

that Cowley at the age of twelve should show the high
flown rhetoric which often disfigures his later writings,

yet in this second poem we find them frequently
appearing while the tenth year production is told
in a simple straight-forward way, and has few unnecessary and ornamental words. We give a few
passages from the poem from Mr. Grosart's edition.

He who acquainte th' others with his moane,
Addes to his friend's grief, but not cures his own.

Constantia's Song.

Time flye with greater speed away,
Adde feathers to thy wings,
Till thy hast in flying brings
That wisht for and expected day.
Comforts sunne wee then shall see
Though at first it darkness bee
With dangers, yet those clouds but gon
Our day will put his lustre on.
Then tho' death's sad night doe come,

---

[1]) "17th Century Studies", Gosse, p. 175.

> And wee in silence sleepe,
> Lasting day agen will grete
> Our ravisht soules, and then there 's none
> Can part us more; no death, nor friends,
> Being dead, their power o'er us ends.
> Thus there 's nothing can dissever
> Hearts which love hath joyn'd together.

"An Elegie" on the death of his cousin, Mr. Clarke, written in his 13th year and "A Dream of Elysium", written perhaps earlier, are much more mature in subject as well as in treatment, than the two poems quoted.

The last couplet of the "Elysium" runs:

> Thus chiefest joyes, glide with the swiftest stream
> And all our greatest pleesure 's but a dream.

These poems all belong to the volume "Poetical Blossoms by A. C." 1633.

In 1636 appeared "Sylva". In this volume is a poem of his 13th year which can rank with the finest in our literature. It may be found, in part, in the Essay on "*Myself*", quoted later on.

Grosart says of the whole poem: "I take it to be felicitously done all thro', alike in warp and woof, matter and form". In Milton's first sonnet 1645 are some lines which Gosse and Grosart think might have reference to Cowley's early productions.

> My hasting dayes flie on with full career,
> But my late spring no *bud or blossom* sheweth.

Cowley's early poems were often reprinted. Before the edition of 1704 the Bookseller says:

> The following poems of Mr Cowley being much enquired after and very scarce (the Town hardly affording one book, tho' it hath been eight times printed) we thought this *ninth* edition could not fail of being well received by the world.

In his sixteenth year Cowley completed "Love's Riddle", a pastoral drama. When he went to Cambridge he carried the manuscript of this poem in his pocket. It was influenced by Randolph's "Jealous Lovers".

"A following without an imitation" according to Gosse. The latter also says of it:

It contains no genuine passion, no knowledge of the phenomena of nature, no observant love of birds or flowers, or the beauties of country life.

Dr Johnson says of it:

This comedy is of the pastoral kind, which requires no knowledge of the living world.

Grosart shows very clearly by citations that Cowley had, even at that tender age, that true love of the beautiful in nature and a power of observation remarkable in a boy of 16.

In the dedication Cowley says:

It is not stuffed with names of Gods, hard words,
Such as the Methamorphosis affords.

This play is written in blank verse and well conducted and concluded.

It was published in 1638 and also a still bolder attempt. A five act Latin Comedy—"Naufragium Joculare" in imitation of Plautus. The name, it is said "prophesied its fate".

The humor shown in this play Grosart thinks remarkable, as humor is a rare element in a child genius. In Ward's English Dramatic Literature, volume II, p. 369, are these lines:

Acted at Trinity in 1638 it obtained celebrity by the boisterous fun of its first act, in which a drunken company are deluded into the belief that they are suffering shipwreck, till their request to be led in *inferiora navis* is summarily complied with.

It was translated in 1705.

At the age of twenty we find Cowley a popular poet, a rising scholar, with an outlook for the future which few have attained during University life. A portrait shows him a handsome youth with long fair curls falling on his shoulders, regular features, and bright intelligent countenance.

His fame Cowley bore with modesty.

In "the Motto", written at an early age, are these lines:

> What shall I do to be for ever known
> And make the age to come my own?
>
> * * *
>
> Unpast Alps stop me, but I'll cut thro' all,
> And march the muses Hannibal.
> Hence all the flattering vanities that lay
> Nets of roses in the way.
>
> * * *
>
> Come my best friends, my books, and lead me on.
> Welcome great Stagirite and teach me now
> All I was born to know.

The Guardian.

In 1641 Prince Charles passed through Cambridge on his way to join his father in York. Cowley was called upon, as the poet of the College, to write a comedy for his entertainment.

The result was the Guardian.

The play was acted before the Prince on March 12th 1641. A letter is preserved which gives the following: [1]

From the Regenthouse His Highness went to Trinity College, where he saw, after dinner, a Comedy, in English

---

[1] Sketch of Cowley's Life, Lumby, p. 19.

and gave all signs of acceptance which he could and more
than the University dared to expect.

The farcical parts of the play were in prose,
but the more important characters spoke in blank
verse. In the Prologue to the first performance
Cowley alludes to the hurried manner in which it
was written:

> Accept our hasty zeal
> A thing that's played ere 'tis a play
> And acted ere 'tis made.

And in the Epilogue:

> Tho' it should fall beneath your mortal scorn
> Scare could it die more quickly than 'twas born.

This was the first appearance of a play which
was destined to have a varied history.

On it alone rests Cowley's right to be placed
among the Dramatists of the 17th Century. Under a
changed name, "Cutter of Coleman Street", it afterwards appeared, and though not at first accepted
finally received applause.

It was not printed until 1650 while its author
was in Paris. This edition was unauthorized and is
now very rare. When Cowley returned to England
he rewrote the play and brought it on the stage
under its new name (1658). Dryden and Sprat went
to see the first performance and related that Cowley
did not bear bravely its failure.

It was considered generally as a satire on the
Kings party. In the preface Cowley defends himself
from this charge. From Grosart we take the following
interesting contemporary notices of the play. An
entry in Downe's Roscius Anglicanus.

This Comedy being acted[1]) so perfectly well and exact,
it was performed a whole week with a full audience.

---

[1]) Grosart's Mem. Introd., p. 26.

It was acted not only at Cambridge but several times afterwards privately during the prohibition of the stage and publicly at Dublin, and always with applause. [1]

1661 December 16. After dinner to the Opera (the Duke's House, or D'avant's Theatre), where there was a new play, "Cutter of Coleman Street" made in the year 1658, with reflections much upon the late times; and it being the first time, the pay was doubled, and so to save my money, my wife and I went into the Gallery, and there sat and saw very well; and a very good play it is. It seems of Cowley's making. [2]

Later—Aug. 5, 1668. To the Duke of York's play-house, and there saw the "Guardian", formerly, the same, I find, that was called "Cutter of Coleman Street"; a silly play.

The following is from Ward: [3]

In the chief characters there is considerable humor. Cutter and Worm are two swaggerers who conceal their vagabond character under cover of their devotion to the good cause. To further their purposes they are quite ready to ruin one another or to perpetrate any horrible deed. Colonel Jolly— tho' his manners are little better than his morals, and his facetious daughter Aurelia are drawn fresh from life. In the sentimental characters, Truman and Lucia, there are touches of pathos from which an inferior hand would have shrunk.

Dr Johnson knows not why it should have been rejected as it "certainly had in a great [4] measure the power of fixing attention and exciting merriment".

Masson thinks:

Cutter of Coleman Street was an absurd [5] ill-tempered thing, coarsely worded, and utterly unworthy of Cowley's genius.

To a reader of the 19th Century the play certainly gives the impression of a satire. A vein of

---

[1] Langbaine's Lives, p. 81.
[2] Pepy's Diary, Bright's Edition 1877, I., 389.
[3] Ward's English Drame, Lib. II., p. 485.
[4] Johnson's Life of Cowley, p. 19.
[5] Masson's Life of Milton, vol. 6, p. 358.

concealed and double meaning seems to run through the entire play and one can easily imagine the Royal party to have taken offence. Imitations of the dramatists of the late Elizabethan period are easily observable.

The Drama was not the field in which Cowley's genius is seen to best avantage. He cannot be said to have had dramatic talent, or a true taste for the Drama, which was at that time so popular. We must agree with Masson in thinking this effusion unworthy of Cowley's genius. It was called forth by the necessity of the occasion. The poet of the College being expected to coin from his brain amusement for every Royal occasion and the "vaulting ambition" of youth feeling itself equal to all demands. In the later years of his quiet retirement Cowley showed the true bent of his genius. He was never again guilty of an attempt in the dramatic field. Shortly after Cowley went to Oxford (1646) appeared a satire from his pen called "The Puritan and the Papist".

This was only inserted in a late collection of his works, it is said, at the earnest request of Dr Johnson.

From Grosart on this subject: [1]

He had libelled truculently and heartlessly under the name *Puritan,* the noblest men and women of the Commonwealth, from the leaders to the Roundhead Commonalty.

Cowley, of course, could have little knowledge of the Puritan except from the side of their enemies, who were totally incapable of doing them justice, even had they wished to do so.

"The Civil War", attributed to Cowley by Dryden in his collection (1716), is considered by Grosart, doubtful.

[1] Mem. Introd., p. 16.

For ourselves, after having read the poems, if they are to be considered Cowley's, we should place them among the writings of which he himself says in his preface to the 1656 edition:[1])

"In all civil discussions, when they break into open hostilities, the war of the pen is allowed to accompany that of the sword, and every one is in a manner *obliged* with his tongue as well as hand to serve and assist one side which he engages in; yet when the event of battel and the unaccountable will of God has determined the controversy and that we have submitted to the conditions of the conqueror, we must lay down our pens as well as arms, we must march out of our cause itself and dismantle *that,* as well as our Towns and Castles, of all the works and fortifications of wit, and Reason by which we defended it. We ought not sure to begin to revive the remembrance of those times and actions for which we have received a general amnesty. The truth is, neither we, nor they ought by the Representations of Places and images to make a kind of artificial memory of those things wherein we are all bound to desire, like Themistocles, the art of oblivion. The enmity of fellow citizens should be like that of lovers—the redintegration of their amity.

The names of Party and titles of division, which are sometimes, in effect, the whole quarrel, should be extinguished and forbidden in peace under the notion of 'Acts of hostility' —and I would have it accounted no less unlawful to rip up old wounds, than to give new ones; which has made me not only abstain from printing anything of this kind, but to burn the very copies, and inflict a severer punishment on them myself, than perhaps the most rigid officer of State would have thought that they deserved."

These lines are those which were suppressed as denoting a diminution of loyalty.

Such an expression of opinion as the above could not fail to bring upon Cowley the suspicion, if not the open enmity, of the Royal party. It was not by men of Cowley's calibre, that the Rebellion

---

[1]) Unmutilated Preface of 1656. Grosart's Mem. Introd., 126.

was fought out. The expression of such opinions, in 1656, as well as the very holding them, gives us a deep insight into Cowley's true character. Pure, just and upright in his own judgments he could not even imagine how such opinion would be received by the very men with whom he had lived in close contact for years. He wrote the words in good faith and would have published them if some more worldly minded friends hat not advised differently.

These lines alone should be sufficient to defend from the charge of mere Hero-worship all that has been said and quoted in these pages in praise of Cowley's character.

In 1648 appeared a satire "The Four Ages of England", and a doggeral called "A Satire against Separatists".

These though printed under Cowley's name were not his. He openly disavowed the former.

The Epic (Davideis).

During the last months of Cowley's residence in Cambridge he was engaged on an Epic poem. The most magnificant flight he had yet attempted.

The preface to the Miscellanies of 1656, which include the Davideis, contains a fine discourse on sacred poetry [1]) which is interesting as having preceded the "Paradise Lost" and Drydens "Prefaces". Grosart calls it historically and critically epochmaking.

The subject which Cowley chose for his Epic was one which was well calculated to arouse the enthusiasm of a youthful poet, the story of David.

---

[1]) Mem. Introd., p. 66.

It is a fragment, only one third of the originally designed work having been completed.

An Epic from a youth of 20 is an interesting phenomenon. Sprat says of this poem:

"His "Davideis" was written at so young an age, that if we shall reflect on the vastness of the argument, and his manner of handling it, he may seem like one of those miracles that he there adorns, like a boy attempting Goliath."

Cowley uses in this poem the heroic verse, varied, however, by occasional Alexandrines. This was new in English verse. "Dryden[1]) imitated it. Pope excluded it from heroic verse." The "Davideis" is divided into twelve books as originally intended; not because of the Tribes but after the pattern of Virgil. Only four of these books were finished, also in imitation of Homer and Virgil. "Poets, says Cowley,[2]) never come to the end of their story but only so near that all can see the end of it."

The opening is Virgilian:

I sing the man who Judah's scepter bore
In that right hand which held the crook before.

Even though I could have done better, he says:[3])

I should not have ventured upon it but follow the custom of antiquity in beginning with a proposition of the whole and an invocation to heaven for assistance.

He boasts of being the first to write what he calls a "divine poem"—at least in *English*. He also imitated Virgil in leaving occasionally half verses.

Cowley did not believe, as Johnson and other critics, that Virgil *did not* purposely leave these lines incomplete. In the invocation occur these remarkably beautiful lines on sacred poetry.

---

[1]) 17th Century Studies. Gosse, 1885, p. 194.

[2]) Cowley's Notes upon the first Book.

[3]) Notes upon the first Book.

Too long the muses land hath heathen been;
Their Gods too long were devils, and virtues, sin;
But thou Eternal Word hast called forth me
The Apostle to convert that world to thee.

*   *   *

So with pure hands thy heavenly fires to take,
My well-changed muse I a chaste vestal make!
From earth's vain joys and loves soft witchcraft free,
I consecrate my Magdelene to thee:
Lo, this great work, a temple to thy praise,
On polished pillars of strong verse I raise!
A temple, where if thou vouchsafe to dwell
It Solomon's and Herod's shall excel.

The scene is laid first in Hell, where the devils are calling for a spirit to tempt Saul. "Are we such nothings that our will can be stopped by a Shepherd boy? Lucifer in this strain calls upon his emissaries for help and finally Envy replies.

She takes one of her worst, her best loved snakes:

Softly, dear worm, soft and unseen (said she)
Into his bosom steal and in it be
My Vice-roy. At that word she took her flight
And her loose shape dissolved into the night.

The work was well done—jealousy was whispered into the ear of Saul. The scene next changes to heaven—to the presence of God himself. *God* he allows to speak in Alexandrines.

God sends an angel to David, who goes to play before Saul, but Saul resists the power of music and attempts to kill David. Then follows a description of the Prophet's College. This description has a wonderfully modern sound. Gosse remarks:[1]

It appears to have been modelled on the University of Cambridge.

---

[1] "17th Century Studies", p. 195.

If one turns to Cowley's notes on this passage he will find the following:

The description looks at first sight as if I had taken the pattern of it from ours at the Universities; but the truth is, ours were formed after the example of the Jews.

To this College David flies for safety after having been assisted in his escape by his wife, who puts a "pale statue" in David's bed and pretends that her husband is sick to death.

So ends the first book. The second opens with lines which recall Chancer:

> But now the early birds began to call
> The morning forth, up rose the sun and Saul.

> Up roos the sonne, and up roos Emelye.
> > Knightes Tale, 1415.

David's absence is the cause of Saul's anger. Jonathan explains the reason, which leads to an exhibition of Saul's anger against Jonathan. He seizes a spear to strike Jonathan, when the latter makes his escape into the forest where he meets his friend.

"A reverent oath of constant love they make." David lies beneath a tree—falls asleep—Fancy visits him causing a dream in which he sees the succession of his race till the birth of Christ.

As he awakes, Gabriel assumes human form and assures him of the truth of his vision.

The description of Gabriel's dress is a good example of Cowley's play of fancy. [1]

> He took for skin a cloud most soft and bright,
> That ere the midday sun pierced thro' with light.

> Upon his cheeks a lively blush he spread;
> Washed from the morning beauties deepest red.
> An harmless flaming meteor shone for hair,
> And fell adown his shoulders with loose care.

---

[1] Cowley's Works, 1700, "Davideis", Bk. 2nd, p. 44.

He cuts out a silk mantle from the skies,
Where the most sprightly azure pleas'd the eyes.
This he with starry vapors spangles all,
Took in their prime e'er they grow ripe and fall.
Of a new rainbow e'er it fret or fade,
The choicest piece took out, a scarf is made.
Small streaming clouds he does for wings display,
Not virtuous lovers' sighs more soft than they.
These he gilds o'er with the suns richest rays
Caught gliding o'er pure streams on which he plays.

In the 3rd book David flees to Nob thence to Gath where he wishes to lie concealed:

Alas! in vain! what can such greatness hide!
Stones of small worth may lie unseen by *day,*
But *night* itself does the rich *Gem* betray.

David pretends madness and escapes to the cave of Adullam.

The cave of Adullam, says Cowley in notes on book third, "still remains and was used by the Christians for their refuge upon several irruptions of the Turks". Among the friends, kindred and servants who came with David, was Asabel, the swift-footed. A sort of Ajax. [1])

Swifter than the northern wind;
Scarce could the nimble motions of his mind
Outgo his feet; so strangely would he run,
That time itself perceived not what was done.

Oft o'er the lawns and meadows would he pass,
His weight unknown and harmless to the grass,
Oft o'er the sands and hollow dust would trace,
Yet no one atom trouble or displace.

Cowley defends himself for this description by quoting the well known passage from Virgil:

---

[1]) Cowley's Works, 1700, "Davideis", Bk. 3rst, p. 56.

Illa vel intactæ segetis per summa volaret
Gramina, nec teneras cursu læsisset aristas.
Vel mare per medium fluctu suspensa tumenti
Ferret iter, celeres nec tingeret æquore plantas.

Eneid 7—808.

The walking over the water, he says, is too
much, yet he took it from Homer. [1]

Scott has a passage, descriptive of fair Ellen,
in the "Lady of the Lake":

> E'en the light Harebell raised its head
> Elastic from her fairy tread.

The Philistins encamp at Dammin. Goliath in-
sults the Israelites. David comes to the camp and
asks Saul's leave to fight the giant.

> Much the rewards propos'd his spirit enflame,
> Saul's daughter much, and much the voice of fame.

The combat and slaughter of Goliath follow.
Then the love story of David. We see the poet and
warrior in the character of a lover. [2]

Saul's Daughters are thus described.

> Like two bright eyes in a fair body placed,
> Saul's royal house two beaut'ous daughters grac'd.
> Merab the first, Michal the younger named,
> Both equally for different glories fam'd.
> Merab with spacious beauty fill'd the sight,
> But too much awe chastis'd the bold delight.
> Like a calm sea, which to th' enlarged view,
> Gives pleasure, but gives fear and rev'rence too.
> Michal's sweet looks clear and free joys did move,
> And no less strong, tho' much more gentle love.
> Merab appear'd like some fair princely tower,
> Michal some virgin Queen's delicious bower.
> A clean and lively brown was Merab's dye,
> Such as the prouder colors might envy.
> Michal's pure skin shone with such taintless white,
> As scattered the weak rays of human sight.

[1] See Notes on Book third.
[2] Cowley's Works, 1700, "Davideis", Bk. III, p. 67.

Her lips and cheeks a nobler red did show,
Than e'er on fruits or flowers Heav'ns pencil drew.
From Merab's eyes fierce and quick lightnings came,
From Michal's the sun's mild yet active flame;
Merab's long hair was glossy chestnut brown,
Tresses of palest gold did Michal crown.
Such was their outward form, and one might find
A difference not unlike it in the mind.
Merab with comely majesty and state
Bore high th'advantage of her worth and fate.
Such humble sweetness did soft Michal show,
That none who reach so high e'er stoopd so low.
Merab rejoiced in her wrackt lovers pain,
And fortified her virtue with disdain.
The grief she caused gave gentle Michal grief,
She wished her beauties less for their relief.
Business and power Merab's large thoughts did vex,
Her wit disdaind the fetters of her sex.
Michal no less disdained affairs and noise,
Yet did it not from ignorance, but choice.
In brief, both copies were more sweetly drawn;
Merab of Saul, Michal of Jonathan. [1])

William Cullen Bryant was the first who expressed the opinion that Scott must have had Cowley's description of Merab and Michal in his mind when he described the two daughters of Magnus Troil Minna and Benda in the "Pirate".

Those who are interested may find the Cowley and Scott descriptions side by side in Grosart. [2])

The day that David great Goliath slew,
Not great Goliath's sword was more his due
Than Merab.

But Merab disdained the obscure youth never before seen at court.

Who Shepherd's staff and Shepherd's habit wore.

---

[1]) Cowley's Works, 1700, "Davideis", Bk. III, p. 69.
[2]) Mem. Introd., p. 67.

David became the suitor of Michal and touched
his faithful Lyre beneath her window.

David's song.

Awake, awake my lyre
And tell thy silent master's humble tale;
In sounds that may prevail;
Sounds that gentle thoughts inspire,
Tho' so exalted she
And I so lowly be,
Tell her such different notes make all thy harmonie.

Hark, how the strings awake,
And tho' the moving hand approach not near
Themselves with awful fear,
A kind of mem'rous trembling make.
Now all thy forces try,
Now all thy charms apply,
Revenge upon her ear the conquest of her eye.

Weak lyre! thy virtue sure
Is useless here, since thou art only found
To cure, but not to wound,
And she to wound, but not to cure.
Too weak too wilt thou prove
My passion to remove,
Physick to other ills, thou 'rt nourishment to love.

Sleep, sleep again, my lyre,
For thou canst never tell my humble tale,
In sounds that will prevail,
Nor gentle thoughts in her inspire;
All thy vain mirth lay by
Bid thy strings silent bee,
Sleep, sleep again, my lyre, and let thy master die.

David's love is thus made known. The consent
of Saul obtained and the marriage and wedding feast
are described.

The relapse of Saul and his terrible persecution
of David follow. With this recital of Joab ends the
third book.

The fourth book opens with a hunt at Nebo .to which Moab invites his guest. During the ride they fall into conversation and Moab desires to know from David the reasons for the change of Government in Israel, how Saul came to the crown &c.

David relates the story of Judges, why the people wished a king. Samuel's reply, full of wisdom: [1]

> You 're sure the first, said he,
> Of free-born men that begged for slavery.
>
>   *   *   *
>
> Cheat not yourselves with words, for tho' a king
> Be the mild name, a Tyrant is the thing.
> Let his power loose, and you shall quickly see
> How mild a thing unbounded man will be.
>
>   *   *   *
>
> Methinks (thus Moab interrupts him here)
> The good old seer 'gainst kings was too severe,
> 'Tis *jest* to tell a people that they 're *free,*
> Who, or how many shall their masters be,
> Is the sole doubt; laws guide but cannot reign;
> And tho' they bind not kings, yet they restrain.

They assemble at the Tabernacle to hear the decision. In describing *Saul* Cowley uses an Alexandrine.

> Like some fair pine o'erlooking all the ignoble wood.

D[r] Johnson irefully asks why a pine looks taller in an Alexandrine than in ten syllables.

Jonathan's conduct in war is described in the following: Then the reverse side of his character. [2]

> In war the adverse troop he does assail
> Like an impetuous storm of wind and hail.
> In peace like gentlest dew that does assuage
> The burning months, and temper Syrius' rage.
>
>   *   *   *

---

[1] Cowley's Works, 1701, p. 86 and 87, "Davideis", Bk. IV.
[2] Cowley's Works, 1700, "Davideis", Bk. IV, p. 91.

His love to friends no bounds or rule does know,
What he to heaven all that to him they owe
Keen as his sword and pointed as his wit;
His judgment, like best armor, strong and fit.
And such an eloquence to both these does join
As makes in both beauty and use combine.

*   *   *

And all these virtues were to ripeness grown,
E'er yet his flower of youth was fully blown.
All autumn's store did his rich spring adorn;
Like trees in paradise he with fruit was born.
Such is his soul; and if, as some men tell,
Souls form and build these mansions where they dwell;
Who'er but sees his body must confess,
The architect no doubt could be no less.

The following couplet cannot fail to recall to every reader of Virgil, his famous verse:

Here with sharp neighs the warlike horses sound;
And with proud prancnigs beat the putred ground.

Quadrupedante putrem sonitu quatit ungula campum.
Eneid VIII, 596.

On consulting Cowley's notes one finds the following:

This is in emulation of the Virgilian verse.

The following description of an army and the defeat forcible recall Homer's celebrated descriptions of the same.

Like fields of corn their armed squadrons stand;
As thick and numberless they hide the land.

*   *   *

Thousands from thence fly scattered every day;
Thick as the leaves that shake and drop away,
When they the approach of stormy winter find
The noole tree all bare expos'd to th' wind.

Milton's well known line is also here recalled: [1]

Thick as autumnal leaves that strew the vale of Vallombrosa.

The fourth book closes with David's relation of the war with the Philistines, and Saul's rash vow by which Jonathan was doomed to death but saved by the people.

Cowley's description of Heaven and Hell might have been read by Milton. The former in his description of Hell lays more stress on darkness and gloom and does not introduce the feature of change from heat to cold as Milton does. In both descriptions of Heaven the "excessive bright" predominates. The touch of a master hand cannot be claimed for Cowley's descriptions. We have none of the misty vagueness—the "seeing thro' a glass darkly" which should accompany descriptions of that which the eye of man hath not seen—the heart of men not conceived. The notes which accompany the "Davideis" deserve praise. They show an amount of reading and research which adds to the wonder and admiration excited by the youthful prodigy. Dr Johnson says of them: [2]

Cowley's critical abilities have not been sufficiently observed. The decisions and remarks which his prefaces and his notes to the "Davideis" supply, were at that time accessions to English literature, and show such skill as raises our wish for more examples.

The last remark suggests the thought that if Cowley's life had been prolonged, the work of his mature years would have been in the direction of criticism.

---

[1] Cowley's Works, 1700, "Davideis", Bk. IV, p. 95.
[2] Johnson's Life of Cowley, p. 37.

Ah, who shall lift the wand of magic power
And the lost clue regain?
The unfinished window in Aladdin's tower,
Unfinished must remain.

The "Davideis" was once quoted by the Spectator and once by Dryden, in "Mac Flecknoe", *imitated*.

Pope consciously or unconseiously seems to have borrowed from Cowley. The lines:

Round the whole earth his dreaded name shall sound,
And reach to worlds that must not yet be found,

from the "Davideis", appear in the Essay on criticism in the following form:

Nations unborn, your mighty names shall sound
And worlds applaud that must not yet be found.

In a paraphrase of one of Horace's Epistles we have from Cowley:

Nor does the roughest season of the sky
Or sullen Jove all sports to him deny,
He runs the mazes of the nimble hare,
His well-mouthed dogs' glad concert rends the air.

These appear in "Windsor Forest" thus:

Nor yet when moist Arcturus clouds the sky,
The woods and fields their pleasing toils deny:
To plains with well-breathed beagles we repair,
And trace the mazes of the circling hare.

Cowper's line:

God made the country, and man made the town [1]).

may perhaps be traced to Cowley's:

God the first garden made, and the first city Cain.

The familiar household phrases:

"If we compare great things with small" and
—„by the bye"—we may trace to Cowley.

---

[1]) Cowper's Lask, Bk. I.

Dryden's "Ode on St. Cecilia's Day" is in direct imitation of Cowley's "Resurrection".

The poem on the "Shortness of Human Life"
might have suggested Longfellow's "Arrow and the
Song"—one passage reads:

> Mark that swift arrow how it cuts the ayre,
> How it outruns the hunting eye
> Use all persuasions now and try
> If thou canst call it back, or stay it there!
> That way it went, but thou shalt find
> No track of't left behind.

Another poem "Poverty to be preferred to dis-
contented Riches"—reminds in one stanza of Wordsworth's "Daffodils".

> Here Lillies wash and grow more white
> And Daffodils to see themselves delight.

Grosart[1]) has given us besides a number of
instances where George Crabbe seems to have been
under the influence of Cowley.

The Mistress.

In 1647 appeared the "Mistress".
Sprat says of it:

If there needed any excuse to be made, that his love-
verses should take up so great a share in his works, it may
be alleged that they were composed when he was very young.
But it is a vain thing to make any apology for that sort of
writings.

*　　*　　*

I only except one or two expressions, which I wish I
could have prevailed with those that had the right of the other
edition to have left out. But of all the rest I dare boldly
pronounce, that never yet so much was written on a subject
so delicate, that can less offend the severest rules of morality.

---

[1]) Mem. Introd., p. 104.

Dʳ Johnson speaks as follows of the poems: [1]

They have all the same beauties and the same faults and nearly in the same proportion.

* * *

Considered as the verses of a lover, no man that ever lived will much commend them. They are neither courtly nor pathetic, have neither gallantry nor fondness. His praises are too far sought, and too hy perbolical, either to express love or to excite it; every stanza is crowded with darts and flames, with wounds and death, with mingled souls and with broken hearts.

* * *

The compositions are such as might have been written for penance by a hermit, or for hire by a philosophical rhymer who had only heard of another sex; for they turn the mind only on the writer, whom, without thinking on a woman but as the subject for his task, we sometimes esteem learned and sometimes despise astrifling, always admire as ingenious, and always condemn as unnatural.

W. C. Bryant says of them: [2]

The 44 poems included under the title of "The Mistress" —have little to recommend them save the ingenuity of which Cowper speaks. Their subject is love and they pursue the metaphors employed by poets to describe that passion, until they may be said to be fairly run down in the chase. There is much skill shown in the exercise of art, and there is no lack of learning, but there is no emotion. If all Cowley's poems had been such, the neglect of which Pope speaks would have been fully deserved.

From Stebbings Essay on Cowley:

The subject quickly made it popular, rather than the merits of the poems. It is not without occasional beauties—at times a turn or a tone is caught which appears an anticipation of Tennyson, but the general impression on the modern reader is laborious monotony.

---

[1] Johnson's Life of Cowley, pp. 39—40.
[2] Bryant in North Amer. Review, Junes 1877, p. 375.

From Gosse the following: [1])

The Mistress was fated to become one of the most admired books of the age. It was a pocket compendium of the science of being ingenious in affairs of the heart; and its purity and scolastic phrases recommended it to many who were no judges of poetry, but very keen censors of morality. To us it is the most unreadable production of its author, dry and tedious, without tenderness, without melancholy, without music.

* * *

All simply dull, overloaded with ingenious, prosaic fancy, and set to eccentric measures of the author's invention, that but serve to prove his metrical ineptitude.

Grosart holds most of these opinions to be not "independent judgments"—D[r] Johnson he thinks would not have been content without contradicting Sprat: [2])

And so we have his labored commonplaces and after critics down to the present age have echoed him. So that I must reiterate, it is traditionary criticism, and not the outcome of personal and earnest study of the poems.

* * *

The real student of the love poems will discern genuine emotion, real passion, and the language of the heart.

"Who shall decide when doctors disagree?"
Cowley says himself of the poems:

Poets are scarce thought freemen of their company without paying some duties, and obliging themselves to be true to love. Sooner or later they must all pass thro' their trial, like some Mohometan monks that are bound by their order, once at least in their life, to make a pilgrimage to Mecca.

For ourselves, finding more to praise than Gosse and less than Grosart, we must confess that Cow-

[1]) "17th Century Studies", p. 184. Londen 1885.
[2]) Mem. Introd., p. 51.

ley's own statement of the origin of the poems finds its corroboration in the same, and we feel inclined to echo the "unreadable" of Gosse and the "laborious monotony" of Stebbing. Cowley seems never to have been really touched by the "divine passion", though we have an unsupported story to the contrary. After all that can be said against the Mistress, one must confess that it contains some gems. One especially „The Wish"—"a delicious well in an arid desert":

> Well then I now do plainly see
> This busy world and I shall ne'er agree;
> The very honey of all earthly joy
> Does of all meats the soonest cloy.
>
> And they, methinks, deserve my pity,
> Who for it can endure the stings,
> The crowd, and buzz and murmurings
> Of this great hive the city.
>
> Ah, yet ere I descend to the grave,
> May I a small house and large garden have!
> And a few friends and many books, both true,
> Both wise and both delightful too!
>
> *   *   *
>
> Oh, fountains, when in you shall I
> Myself, eas'd of unpeaceful thoughts espy?
> Oh fields! oh woods! when, when shall I be made
> The happy tenant of your shade?
> Here's the spring-head of pleasure's flood;
> Where all the riches lie that she
> Has coined and stampt for good.

The Miscellanies, 1656.

In 1656 appeared a volume in small folio—"The Works of A. Cowley." It contained many poems not before printed.

These Miscellanies were compositions which extended over many years. The finest poems in the volume are the elegies on his friends William Harvey and Richard Crashaw. The latter had been Cowley's friend at Cambridge, had been expelled with him for the same reason, had been assisted by Cowley and later had gone to Italy. In Italy, through the assistance of Queen Henrietta Maria and Lord Jermyn, he had received a position in Loreto, where he died in 1649.

As Crashaw was a Roman Catholic, Cowley braved much criticism in his noble act of fidelity to his friend at a time when scarce another voice in all England was raised to honor him.

> Poet and Saint! to thee alone are given
> The two most sacred names of earth and heaven.
> The hard and rarest union which can be
> Next that of Godhead with humanity.
>
>   *   *   *
>
> His faith perhaps in some nice tenets might
> Be wrong; his *life,* I'm sure, was in the right.
> And I myself a Catholic will be
> So far, at least, great saint, to pray to thee
> Hail bard triumphant! and some care bestow
> On us the poets militant below!
>
> Thou from low earth in nobler flames didst rise,
> And like Elijah mount alive the skies.
> Elisha-like—but with a wish much less,
> More fit thy greatness and my littleness—
> Lo, here I beg—I whom thou once didst prove
> So humble to esteem, so good to love—
> Not that thy spirit might on me doubled be,
> I ask but *half* thy mighty spirit for me.
> And when my muse soars with so strong a wing,
> I will learn of things divine, and first of thee to sing.

William Harvey had also been a Cambridge friend and was suddenly called away.

Cowley sings of him:

My dearest friend, would I had died for thee![1]
Life and this world henceforth will tedious be.

       *   *   *

He was my friend, the truest friend on earth.

       *   *   *

Say, for you saw us, ye immortal lights,
How oft unwearied have we spent the nights?
Till the Ledean stars so fam'd for love,
Wondered at us from above.

       *   *   *

Ye fields of Cambridge, our dear Cambridge, say,
Have ye not seen us walking every day?
Was there a tree about which did not know
    The love betwixt us two?
Henceforth, ye gentle trees, forever fade;
    Or your sad branches thicker join,
    And into darker shades combine;
Dark as the grave wherein my friend is laid.

       *   *   *

And if the glorious saints cease not to know
Their wretched friends who fight with life below;
Thy flame to me does still the same abide,
    Only more pure and rarified.
There whilst immortal hymns thou dost rehearse,
    Thou dost with holy pity see
    Our dull and earthly poesie.
Where grief and misery can be joined with verse.

These two elegies are well worthy to rank with "Lycidas" and the later — "Adonais" and "In Memoriam".

The poem called "The Chronicle" has divided[2] the critics.

---

[1] Cowley's Works, 1700, p. 23.
[2] Cowley's Works, 1700, p. 14.

It is a "*Chronicle*" of flirtations almost too long for any one man's life to have compassed.

We should call it with Gosse an amusing "Jeu d'esprit". It roused the enthusiasm of the great "Moralist" himself—is called by Stebbing (who evidently took it quite earnestly) "sparkling but scandalous"—by Grosart characterized as "incomparable" and gave rise to the following amusing lines of Mary Russell Mitford: [1])

The Chronicle was written 200 years ago, ladies, dear ladies, if we could be sure that no *man* would open this book, if we were all together in (female) parliament assembled, without a single male creature within hearing, might we not acknowledge that the sex, especially that part of it formerly called coquette and now known by the name of *flirt,* is very little altered since the days of the "Merry Monarch"? and that a similar list compiled by some bachelor of Belgravia might, allowing for the difference of custom and of costume, serve very well as a companion to Cowley's Catalogue—I would not have a *man* read this admission for the world.

Anacreontics.

At the end of the folio of 1656 were printed twelve translations or imitations of the Odes of Anacreon. These were in the iambic measure either seven or eight syllables but always of four cadences which Milton used in his minor poems and in "Comus".

Among these poems are "The Grasshopper", "The swallow", and "Gold", three poems which are known to every school-girl. The Anacreons are lively and sparkling and have been much praised. Dr Johnson says of them: [2])

---

[1]) Recollections of a Literary Life, p. 5—8—60.
[2]) Johnson's "Life of Cowley", p. 59.

These little pieces will be found more finished in their kind than any other of Cowley's works. The diction shows nothing of the mould of time, and the sentiments are at no great distance from our present habitudes of thought. Real mirth must be always natural, and nature is uniform. Men have been wise in many different modes; but they have always *laughed* the same way.

Bryant says of the Anacreons:

Even those who have never read anything else that he has written, are familiar with the most felicitous of these, the "Grasshopper". They are but few in number—11 in all, but they surpass the Greek originals.

Grosart thinks "it was these (mainly) that Sprat must have had before him, in his eulogy of Cowley as translator"—in the following:

He has been wonderfully happy in translating many difficult parts of the noblest poets of antiquity . . . . . . This way of leaving verbal translations and chiefly regarding the sense and Genius of the author, was scarce heard of in England before this present age. I will not presume to say that Mr. Cowley was the absolute inventor of it.

Pindarics.

In the Pindarics Cowley made what has been called a "dangerous innovation". Being, as Sprat says, alone with Pindar in a solitary place, in his exile probably, he was set thinking of this style of poetry. Dr Johnson who had no patience with such irregular verse says:[1]

This lax and lawless versification so much concealed the deficiencies of the barren, and flattered the laziness of the idle, that it immediately overspread our books of poetry; all the boys and girls caught the pleasing fashion, and they that could do nothing else could write like Pindar. The rights of antiquity were invaded, and disorder tried to break into the

---

[1] Johnson's "Life of Cowley", p. 73.

Latin even. Pindarism prevailed above half a century; but at last died gradually away, and other imitations supply its place.

Sprat gives the Pindarics his highest praise and says if any are displeased with them they contend not with Cowley but Pindar.

In his preface to the Odes Cowley himself says:

I am in great doubt whether they will be understood by most readers, nay even by very many who are well enough acquainted with the common roads and ordinary tracks of poesy. The figures are unusual and bold even to temerity, and such as I durst not have to do withal in any other kind of poetry: the numbers are various and irregular, and sometimes, especially some of the long ones, seem harsh and uncouth, if the just measures and cadences be not observed in the pronunciation. So that almost all their sweetness and numerosity, which is to be found, if I mistake not, in the roughest if rightly repeated, lies in a manner wholly at the mercy of the reader.

They, at any rate, became very popular and had hosts of imitators.

In the following century the odes of Gray and Collins were closely modelled on the ancient style. In our own times Keats, Shelley and Swinburne, and later still Lowell, have all written odes. Pope only once deviated from his regular classicism. This was his attempt to imitate Dryden's great ode. From Dryden to our own time almost every critic has given Cowley as the introducer of the Pindaric into English poetry—yet we have the Ode of Ben Jonson on the death of Sir H. Morrison. Jonson's ode was true to the ancient model, while Cowley's were irregular. We shall now allow Cowley to speak again for himself:

There are none of Pindar's Dithyrambics extant. They were hymns in honor of Bacchus. It was a bold, free, enthusiastic kind of poetry as of one inspired by Bacchus.

In one of his odes he thus describes the Pindaric:

'T is an unruly and hard mouthed horse
Fierce and unbroken yet,
Impatient of the spur or bit;
Now prances statily and anon flies o'er the plain,
Disdains the servile law of any settled pace,
'T will no unskilled touch endure,
But flings writer and reader too that sits not sure.

Congreve says:

The beauties of Mr. Cowleys verses are an atonement for the irregularity of his stanzas, and though he did not imitate Pindar in the structure of his numbers, he very often happily copied him in the force of his figures and sublimity of his style and sentiments.

Jacobs, a German critic, says of Pindar:

Ein schwacher Zug aus dem Becher, in welchem dieser Dichter den Wein seiner Gesänge mischt, erfüllt mit ungegründeter Missachtung oder unverständigem Staunen; wem es um ein Urteil zu thun ist, der muss ihn ganz ausleeren.

Gifford makes the following remarks on Cowley's Pindarics: [1])

Cowley mistook the very nature of Pindar's poetry, at least of such as is come down to us, and was led away by the ancient allusions to those wild and wonderful strains of which not a line has reached us. The meter of Pindar was regular, that of Cowley is utterly irregular.

In spite of the critics the ode became extremely popular. If a poet felt cramped and constrained by the strict measure of the heroic couplet, he need not to

Bridle in his struggling muse with pain
Which longs to launch into a bolder strain.

He could simply take refuge under the Pindaric and still be "classical and polite". Cowley thus asserts his liberty:

---

[1]) Gifford's "Life of Jonson", vol. II, p. 8.

If life should a well-orderd poem be—
In which he only hits the white
Who joins true profit with the best delight;
The more heroic strain let others take,
Mine the Pindaric way I'll make;
The matter shall be grave, the numbers loose and free;
It shall not keep one settled pace of time,
Nor shall each day just to its neighbor rhyme.
A thousand liberties it shall dispense
And yet shall manage all without offense
Or to the sweetness of the sound, or greatness of the sense.

The much discussed Pindarics of Cowley are fifteen in number; two are paraphrases of Pindar himself—the second Olympic and the first Nemean. Of the former Johnson says: [1])

It is above the original in elegance, and the conclusion below in strength.

Two of the odes are on scriptural subjects, one is an imitation of Horace and the others are entirely original.

Cowley's Latin.

Cowley's translations are not very numerous. Sprat says he had a perfect mastery of Latin, but kept it at a just distance from his English and so his Latin did not make his English too old, nor his English make his Latin too modern.

He says on this subject: [2])

In his Latin poems he has expressed to admiration, all the numbers of verses, and figures of poetry, that are scattered up and down among the ancients. There is hardly to be found in them all any good fashion of speech or color of measure, but he has comprehended it and given instances of it; according as his several arguments required either a majestic spirit, or a passionate or a pleasant. This is the more extraordinary,

---

[1]) Johnson's "Life of Cowley", p. 64.
[2]) Sprat's Life of Cowley, Edition of 1700.

in that it was never yet performed by any single poet of the ancient Romans themselves.

Cambridge University produced about the same time three classical scholars Milton, Cowley and May.

The first two, though so different in genius and opposite in political opinions, concurred in the cultivation of Latin poetry. The English, until this time, had not been able to contest this palm with other nations; it was now able to boast of three classical scholars. D[r] Johnson thinks if Milton and Cowley be compared in their Latin performances, the advantage will lie on Cowley's side. " Milton ", he says: [1]

is generally content to express the thoughts of the ancients in their language; Cowley, without much loss of purity or elegance, accomodates the diction of Rome to his own conceptions.

Cowley's translation of the celebrated ode of Horace, "Quis multa gracilis te puer in rosa" (odes of Horace 1—5), is held, by the critics, to be finer than Milton's. The fourth book of the Davideis Cowley turned into Latin and his poems on plants were written in Latin.

Under the head of "Cowley at the Restoration", in the Academy for 1893, n° 1118, appeared some letters taken from the Carte MS. in the Bodleian Library. The first of these is from Cowley to the Marquis of Ormonde, dated Paris 1659. It is a letter of apology for having said anything which could be construed as an offence to His Majesty, and alleging he had made it the business of his life to uphold His Majesty's person and interests.

The Marquis answers him from Brussels in the following January recommending him to find means

---

[1] Johnson's "Life of Cowley", p. 17.

to say to the King what he had said in his letter
and to make a frank recantation of any sentence of
his which could be wronghy taken, as the King was
not wanting in clemency.

Then follows a letter from Ormonde to Jermyn,
interceding for Cowley. In Jermyn's reply he says
Cowley is a fit subject for the Kings forgiveness and
thanks Ormonde for his expressed interest in Cowley.

Cowley again to the Marquis saying he dare not
write to His Majesty but begs that Ormonde will
say something in his behalf better than he could say
for himself. He then adds he hopes to kiss His
Majesty's hand about a month hence.

These letters are interesting though throwing
no new light on the subject. Cowley in a preface
to which we have already referred, defined his position clearly and seemed to consider it an absurdity
that he could forsake the court in prosperity when
he had been faithful through so many years of ad-
versity.

Odes on the Restoration.

In 1660 Cowley published his ode on "His Majesty's Restoration" and "Return", a long Pindaric.
It is "bombastic and rhetorical" but, for the times,
not so grovelling in its attitude as those of Davenant
and Dryden. The following lines are from Davenant's: [1])

> Thus showing what you are, how quickly we
> Infer what all your subjects soon will be!
> For from the monarch's virtue subjects take
> The ingredient which does public virtue make!
> At his bright beam they all their tapers light,
> And by his dial set their motion right.

---

[1]) Masson's "Life of Milton", vol. 6th, p. 18th.

The following from Dryden's: [1]

How shall I then begin or where conclude
To draw a fame so truly circular?
For in a round what order can be showed,
Where all the parts so equal perfect are.

His grandeur he derived from Heaven alone;
For he was great ere fortune made him so,
And was, like mists that rise against the sun,
Made him but greater *seem,* not greater grow.

And yet dominion was not his design;
We owe that blessing not to him but Heaven,
Which to fair acts unbought rewards did join,
Rewards that less to him than us were given.

The most fulsome passage in Cowley's is the
following: [2]

Will peace her halcyon nest venture to build
Upon a shore with shipwrecks filled?
And trust that sea, where she can hardly say,
Sh' has known these trenty years one calmy day?
Ah! wild and galless dove,
Which do'st the pure and candid dwellings love,
Canst thou in Albion still delight?
Still canst thou think it white?
Will ever fair religion appear
In these deformed ruins? will she clear
The Augean stables of her churches here?

Much may be excused to Cowley, says Masson: [3]

A man of far finer intellect and more generous nature
than Waller, and whose "compliance" had been the effect
of a momentary despair.

Waller came "skipping back" to court at the
Restoration and when asked by Charles II. why the
ode on Cromwell was better than the one on him-

[1] Masson's "Life of Milton", vol. 6th, Dryden's lines.
[2] Cowley's Works, 1700, p. 15, "Ode on His Majesty's Return".
[3] Masson's "Life of Milton", vol. 6th, p. 13.

self, replied with the readiness of repartee which made him the "darling of the House of Commons", "Poets, Sire, succeed better in fiction than in truth".

Davenant had been poet laureate of the late reign—having succeeded Johnson in 1637 and much was expected of him. But how can the "noble John" Dryden be defended, who had fully acknowledged the principles of the commonwealth and had an official position under Thurloe for Oliver, and whose best poem had been his stanzas on Oliver from which the lines above quoted are taken.

Prose works.

Cowley's prose works are justly classed with the best English prose. They form in their style a direct contrast to his poetry. Simple and natural, without a trace of the profuse ornamentation which so often disfigures his poetry.

The oft quoted remark of Dr Johnson:

Whoever wishes to form an English style familiar but not coarse, elegant but not ostentatious must give his days and nights to the volumes of Addison—

might with equal propriety be applied to Cowley's prose. His prose was the production of the years of his retirement after he had gained his reputation as a poet.

Dr Johnson on the prose:

No author ever kept his verse and his prose at a greater distance from each other. His thoughts are natural and his style has a smooth and placid equability, which has never yet obtained its due commendation. Nothing is far-sought, or hard-labored, but all is easy without feebleness, and familiar without grossness.

Mary Mitford says of the Essays: [1])

All too short and all too few, which, whether for thought or for expression have rarely been excelled by any writer in any language. They are eminently distinguished for the grace, the finish and the charms which his verse two often wants.

Grosart says on the same Essays: [2])

I place these only a little beneath the Essays of Bacon for weight and worth, and if it be not literary treason to say so, far above the brilliant essays of your sensational writers of the day. It is like a walk in the greenwood along a tree-shaded river's bank to commune with the prose of Cowley.

There is a naturalness, an artlessness a freshness, a directness, and a wholesomeness about it that is as nurturing as it is exhilarating, and as delightful as inspiring. It augurs a man to be ill furnished, however otherwise learned he may be, if he is not familiar with the warbled prose of the recluse of Chertsey.

When Boswell mentioned to D[r] Johnson the saying of Shenstone that Pope had the art beyond any other writer of condensing sense, Johnson replied:

It is not true, Sir, there is more sense in a line of Cowley than in a page of Pope.

Cowley had planned two prose works which he left unfinished. One of these was on "style", the other on the "Primitive Church".

He was persuaded by many friends to delay his proposed retirement to the country, and by one advised to wait until he had accumulated an estate which might afford him "cum dignitate Otium". To this friend is addressed his essay on "Procrastination". It is a mixture of grave earnestness and playful

---

[1]) Recollections of a Lit. Life, p. 45.
[2]) Mem. Introd., p. 107.

humor with which he combats his friend's advice of
"festina lente".

He quotes from Horace, ever ready on this subject with his "Carpe diem" and "labuntur anni".
It has been said that Cowley "asserted his freedom
in translation and spread his wings so boldly that
he left his author far behind him". Here is a good
example of his power so to do;

Sapere aude;
Incipe; vivendi recte qui prorogat horam,
Rusticus expectat, dum labitur amnis, at ille
Labitur, et labetur in omne volubilis ævum.

Horace, Ep. 1, 2—40.

Begin, be bold, and venture to be wise;
He who defers this work from day to day,
Does on a river's bank expecting stay,
Till the whole stream, which stopt him, should be gone,
That runs, and as it runs, forever will run on.

And in the same essay we have the following:

Jam cras histernum consumpsimus; ecce aliud cras
Egerit hos annos.
Our yesterday's to-morrow now is gone,
And still a new to-morrow does come on;
We by to-morrows draw up all our store,
Till the exhausted well can yield no more.

He so combats his friend's arguments and play-
fully tells him, at the end, that he is even with him
in his classical quotations, but if he should draw
upon *all* his forces from Seneca, Plutarch &c., he could
completely overwhelm him with arguments forcible
and cogent for deferring no longer his retirement.

A short essay on the shortness of life and un-
certainty of riches is a companion piece to the last.
The ever recurring Horatian advice finds a fitting
place here, also:

Spatio brevi
Spem longam reseces.

Vitæ summa brevis spem nos vetat inchoare longam.

This essay closes with a poem which shows Cowley in his lyric glory.

The last stanza runs:

> The wise example of the heavenly lark,
>   Thy fellow-poet, Cowley, mark;
> Above the clouds, let thy proud music sound
>   Thy humble nest build on the ground.

In the essay on "Solitude" he says:

There is no saying shocks me so much as that which I hear often, that a man does not know how to pass his time. 'Twould have been but ill spoken by Methusalem in the nine hundred sixty ninth year of his life; so far it is from us who have not time enough to attain to the utmost perfection of any part of any science, to have cause to complain that we are forced to be idle for want of work.

This Essay closes with a poem of twelve stanzas which has a Wordsworthian ring in its descriptions of the silence and loveliness of nature.

Poets, he says in "Essay on Agriculture", were ever the most faithful and affectionate friends of country life. Poetry was born among shepherds.

> As well might *corn* as verse in cities grow:
> In vain the thankless glebe we plow and sow,
> Against the unnatural soil in vain we strive,
> 'Tis not a ground in which these plants will thrive.

Poetry is delightfully mingled with prose in all of Cowley's Essays. He quotes here from the classics in praise of country life the well known Ode of Horace "Beatus ille qui procul negotiis"—"The Country Mouse" from the same and finally a translation from his own "De Plantarum" for which he makes a humble apology.

"The Garden," one of the gems of Cowley's Prose, is inscribed to Mr J. Evelyn.

Much of the essay is in Cowley's best style of poetry.

The following lines are truly Wordsworthian. Grosart calls them *"priceless"*.

> Where does the wisdom and the power divine
> In a more bright and sweet reflection shine?
> Where do we finer strokes and colors see
> Of the creator's real poetry
> Than when we with attention look
> Upon the third day's volume of the book?
> If we could open and intend our eye,
> We all, like Moses, should expy
> Ev'n in a bush the radiant Diety.

We are here reminded of a similar passage in Browning:

> Earth's crammed with heaven
> And every common bush afire with God,
> But only he who *sees* takes off his shoes,
> The rest sit round it and pluck *blackberries*.

Grosart says of this Essay:[1)]

It will scarcely seem credible that Mr. J. H. Ward, M. A., in his "Selections from English Poets"[2)] says: "In the poem on the Garden Cowley sinks to his lowest." After this who would give a *pinch* of *snuff* for such an Editor's judgment on anything literary? None the less is the "Selections" a welcome and delightful though a most unequal and inadequate work.

In the Essay on "Greatness" Montaigne is quoted as saying, "since we cannot attain to greatness let us have our revenge by railing at it". It gives many apt quotations from the ancients and

---

[1)] Mem. Introd., p. 105.
[2)] Ward's "Selections", II, 243.

ends with the ever ready Horace in his ode "Odi profanum vulgus et arceo".

> Hence ye profane; I hate ye all
> Both the great vulgar, and the small.

Cowley's Essay, "Of Myself", is one of the most unique and original of which our literature can boast. It is an autobiographical sketch, but all too short—we wish for more in the same strain.

It is a hard and nice thing for a man to write of himself; it grates his own heart to say anything of disparagement, and the reader's ears to hear anything of praise from him. There is no danger from me of offending him in that kind; neither my mind, nor my body, nor my fortune, allow me any materials for that vanity. It is sufficient for my own contentment, that they have preserved me from being scandalous, or remarkable on the defective side.

*   *   *

As far as my memory can return back into my past life, before I knew, or was capable of guessing, what the world, or the glories or business of it, were, the natural affections of my soul gave me a secret bent of aversion from them, as some plants are said to turn away from others, by an antipathy imperceptible to themselves, and inscrutable to men's understanding. Even when I was a boy, very young at school, instead of running about on holydays and playing with my fellows, I was wont to steal from them, and walk into the fields, either alone with a book, or with some one companion, if I could find any of the same temper. I was then, too, so much an enemy to all constraint, that my masters could never prevail on me by any persuasions or encouragements, to learn without book the common rules of grammar; in which they dispensed with me alone, because they found I made a shift to do the usual exercise out of my reading and observation. That I was then of the same mind as I am now (which, I confess, I wonder at myself) may appear by the latter end of an ode, which I made when I was but thirteen years old, and which was then printed with my other verses. The beginning of it is boyish; but of this part, which I here set down, I should hardly now be much ashamed.

This only grant me, that my means may lie
Too low for envy, for contempt too high,
    Some honor I would have,
Not from great deeds, but good alone;
The unknown are better, then ill known;
    Rumor can ope the grave.
Acquaintance I would have, but when 't depends
Not on the number, but the choice of friends.

Books should, not business, entertain the light,
And sleep, as undisturbed as death, the night.
    My house a cottage more
Than palace; and should fitting be
For all my use, no luxurie.
    My garden planted o'er
With nature's hand, not arts'; and pleasures yield,
Horace might envy in his Sabine field.

Thus would I double my lifes fading space;
For he, that runs it well, twice runs his race.
    And in this true delight,
These unbought sports, that happy state,
I would not fear, nor wish my fate;
    But boldly say each night,
To-morrow let my sun his beams display
Or, in clouds hide them; I have liv'd to-day.

You may see by it, I was even then acquainted with the poets (for the conclusion is taken from Horace); and perhaps it was the immature and immoderate love of them, which stampt first, or rather engraved, the characters in me: they were like letters cut into the bark of a young tree, which with the tree still grow proportionably.

He closes the essay with the following:

    Nec vos, dulcissima mundi
Nomina, vos Musæ, libertas, otia. libri,
Hortique sylvæque, anima remanente, relinquam.

    Nor by me e'er shall you,
You of all names the sweetest, and the best,
You Muses, books, and liberty, and rest,
You gardens, fields, and woods, forsaken be,
As long as life itself forsakes not me.

Elsewhere, in the same essay, are the lines which should not be passed. They belong to a longer poem which already has been partly quoted, and which originally formed part of the "Mistress". In regard to his cherished solitude, he says:

> I should have then this only fear,
> Lest men, when they my pleasures see,
> Should hither throug to live like me,
> And so make a city here.

On "Liberty", he says:

The liberty of a people consists in being governed by laws which they have made themselves, under whatsoever form it be of government; the liberty of a private man, in being master of his own time and actions, as far as may consist with the laws of God, and of his Country.

The celebrated Ode upon liberty is inserted in this essay. We have already quoted from it and will add these lines:

> In all the freeborn nations of the air,
> Never did bird a spirit so mean and sordid bear,
> As to exchange a native liberty
> Of soaring boldly up into the sky,
> His liberty to sing, to perch, or fly,
> When, and wherever he thought good,
> And all his innocent pleasures of the wood,
> For a more plentiful or constant food.
> Nor ever did ambitious rage
> Make him into a painted cage,
> Or the false forest of a well-hung room,
> For honor and preferment, come.

*   *   *

> Where honor, or where conscience does not bind,
> No other law shall shackle me;
> Slave to myself I will not be,
> Nor shall my future actions be confined
> By my own present mind.

Who by resolves and vows engaged does stand
  For days, that yet belong to fate,
Does like an unthrift, mortgage his estate,
  Before it falls into his hand;
  The bondman of the cloister so
All that he does receive, does always owe;
And still, as time comes in, it goes away
  Not to enjoy, but debts to pay.

Says Emerson:

A foolish consistency is the hobgoblin of little minds, speak what you think to-day in hard thoughts, to-morrow, speak what you think in hard thoughts, tho'it contradict every thing you say to-day.

We would fain hear more, from Cowley, on the liberty "of a people" which he so lightly and skilfully touches in the early part of his essay, but England in the reign of the second Charles was not favorable to the free expression of opinion on this subject. Cowley may flatter himself for his independence and hatred of a "foolish consistency", but for those who read between the lines of his later writings, the conviction will ever arise that his early opinions were much modified after the experience of the *"blessed Restoration"* of monarchy.

It is surely interesting to hear what Cowley will say on the subject of *"Obscurity"*—Cowley who was a popular poet at twenty. He quotes his favorite Horace as commending those who live and die without notice of the world. Then expresses the opinion that the pleasantest condition of life is in *"incognito"*.

What a rare privilege it is to be free from all contentions, from all envying or being envied.—It is a very delightful pastime for two friends to travel up and down together, in places where they are by nobody known, nor know any body. It was the case of Eneas and his friend

Achates, when they walked invisibly about the fields and streets of Carthage:

> A veil of thickened air around them cast,
> That none might know, or see them, as they past.

*   *   *

The erection of a "Philosophical College" was much debated by Cowley and his friends, Evelyn, Boyle, Davenant, and others. The plan was one which Bacon had suggested in his "Advancement of Learning". The object was for the promotion of experimental knowledge, or the study of nature more especially. Cowley complains, justly, that the times, since Aristotle, had been little productive in natural science and the Universities, having been founded in those times, he says, are defective in their constitution as to this way of learning which was not then thought of. Cowley drew up a plan for the building and management of a College, such as mentioned. Some of his ideas are interesting in the light of modern times.

The College should be situated within three miles of London, and if possible upon the side of the river, or near it. The revenue should be £ 4000 a year. 20 Philosophers or Professors. 16 young scholars, servants to the Professors. A Chaplain. Then a number of lower offices are named down to the women who keep the house clean. From the revenue each Professor was to have £ 120 annually and the Chaplain the same sum. To the scholars £ 10 annually each. For the government of the College, a Chancellor or President, and eight Governors should be chosen. The filling vacant Professorships should lie with these. Of the 20 Professors, 4 should be travelling always—each leaving a deputy to supply his place. These travelling Professors should be assigned to the four parts of the world, Europe, Asia, Africa and America. They should take a solemn oath never to write anything to the College, but what after diligent examination they shall fully believe to be true, and to confess and recant it as soon as they find themselves in error.

*   *   *

If any should be author of an invention that may bring in profit, the third part of it shall belong to the inventor, and the remainder to the society. The school shall be divided into 4 classes, not as others are ordinarily into 6 or 7. A method should be established for infusing knowledge and language at the same time. In Latin he recommends Varro, Cato, Pliny, parts of Celsus and Seneca, parts of Cicero, Virgil's Georgics, Grotius' Manilius. Because we want good poets, those who have purposely treated of the solid and the learned, —one book ought to be compiled of all the scattered little parcels among the ancient poets that might serve for the advancement of natural sciences. To this he would add the morals and rhetoric of Cicero and the institutions of Quintilian.

For the Greek they may study Nicander, Oppianus, Aristotle's history of animals; Theophrastus and Dioscorides of plants. For morals and rhetoric Aristotle may suffice, or Hermogenes and Longinus be added for the latter. They should be shewed anatomy as a divertisement—the same method with plants.

They should be taught to declaim in Latin and English as the Romans did in Greek and Latin. All this without any emulation or driving by severity or punishment or terror.

It need scarcely be said the Utopian schemes of Cowley and his friends came to naught.

Cowley's "Discourse by way of vision concerning the Government of Oliver Cromwell" is one of the curiosities of Literature. He has managed the thing so adroitly that Cromwell's best friends cannot wish a better eulogy, a more correct delineation of the traits which characterized Oliver, and on the other hand his enemies may find all the denunciations which their hearts desire. A vein of irony seems to pervade the whole, and we cannot refrain from thinking, as we read, that the pretended irony may

be a cover for the expression of genuine admiration.
The Royalists could not be very enthusiastic in their
admiration of a production so equivocal, where every
expression of censure was accompained by something which sounded much like epithets of a sincere
admirer. A finer picture of the national glories which
England attained under the great Protector, and a
finer description of Cromwell's character were never
given than in this mysteriously worded composition.

When all the liquid world was one extended Thames,

sounds strangely like a satire when applied to the
England of Cowley's childhood, and the lines:

Let rather Roman come again,
Or Saxon, Norman, or the Dane:
In all the bonds we ever bore,
We grieved, we sighed, we wept, we never *blushed* before.

might surely apply to the reigns of the first and
second Charles better than to that of Cromwell.

It is said that Hume has, with the change of a
few words, openly used a passage from this essay
for a panegyric. In this essay Cowley is both the
defender and the reviler of Cromwell, as the defender
is a supposed angel who speaks to him in a vision.
—On the day of Cromwell's funeral, meditating on his
wonderful history, he falls into this vision or dream.

Having both sides of the argument in his hands,
he has evidently tried to outdo himself, and has
succeeded, as all will admit the angel has, in almost
every point, the convincing side of the argument.
The essay ends by the young Charles appearing in
a cloud of glory, and the disappearance of the angel
before him.

Charles' appearance is thus described:

If gold may be compared with angel's hair.

And his decorations:

Across his breast an azure ribbon went

*   *   *

And from his mantle side there shone afar,
A fix't and I believe a real star.

After the recital of Cromwell's glorious achieve-
ments—how insipid and flat fall these descriptions
and praise of the beauty of Charles on the reader's ear.

The prose works of Cowley have been made
more accessible to modern readers by the work of
Rev. J. Rawson Lumby D. D. who published in 1887
"Cowley's Prose Works" with notes and sketch of
the poets life.

In the Academy for 1887, p. 337, appeared a
rather severe criticism on this work. The writer
accuses Lumby of adding to the work only extremely
dry and uninteresting scientific notes. These same
notes we must plead guilty to having read with
great interest.

He thinks Lumby should have said more of the
man and of the age &c.

The Book, in our judgment, has fulfilled its
mission—that of putting the beautiful prose of Cowley
in a cheap and accessible form for modern readers.

A criticism of the man and the age would have
given the work proportions which would have placed
it on a level with the works in which the prose of
Cowley has been hitherto found, and which cannot
be, in any sense, called cheap and accessible.

Dr Johnson gives it as his opinion that if Cowley
was formed by nature for one kind of writing more
than another, his power seems to have been greatest
in the familiar and the festive. No true admirer of
Cowley will agree with the great Coryphæns of

his century in this opinion. Johnson's well known dislike to lyric and descriptive poetry, and his total lack of enthusiasm color his life of Cowley as well as those of Milton and Gray. Friendship and Poetry are surely the subjects on which Cowley's muse has made its most transcendent flights—"high as ever poet mounted".

"Against Hope", "For Hope".

The odes to "Crashaw" and to "Harvey", the elegies on "Sir Henry Wooten" and on "Sir Antony Vandyke"—the ode to the "Royal Society"—"The Hymn to Light"—"To Lord Falkland"—"The Resurrection"—"The Muse"—"Ode to Liberty"—these are the poems which have made his name, on "fame's eternal bead-roll, worthy to be filed." The fault which marred so many of Cowley's lines was his use of fantastic and often obscure comparisons and allusions. He has often been accused of unblushing plagiarism also. Both of these can be excused by a consideration of the prevailing taste of the age in which he lived.

The first was mainly due to the expiring, though still potent, euphuism of the Elizabethan age.

The second—imitation—both in style and subject, was the fashion of the 17th Century. By Cowley always acknowledged without an excuse. Sprat says:

His rough verse was his *choice* not his fault, that he affected a variety to divert mens minds.

No poet was ever more influenced by the age in which he lived than Cowley. That age was one of imitation and artificiality. The court fashions ruling and predominating. This court life, into which he was thrown by the chances of war, had the effect of partly, at least, petrifying, what might have been the poet of nature into a court poet. At times, however, we find him soaring aloft, breaking through the trammels of custom and conventionality—and boldly asserting his right to think and speak in a fashion new to his times and not in accordance with the fashion of courts. These are the productions of which Grosart says:[1])

Those poems which were the outcome of the heart, in which intellect and imagination wrought through his affections, are his most enduring. In this department of our poetical literature, I pronounce Cowley to hold a unique place. I cannot think of a second to be named with him; for Lycidas stands apart.

Perhaps we of this age cannot fully appreciate the boldness and independence required in a poet thus to set at defiance the unwritten law of poetical dictatorship.

The sneers and derision of the court of Charles II. were something not to be braved except by one who, like Cowley, had attained the position of "Sovereign of letters".—It seems a cruel fate which threw an ideal man of letters in the turmoil of civil war. In another Century we can imagine Cowley a truer "Lady of Shalott" than Hawthorn or even Tennyson himself. In the 19th Century he might have vied with Wordsworth as the poet of nature. Grosart names one of the characteristics of Cowley "Wordsworthian *Seeingness* towards nature." Arthur Clough says:

I have bought a Cowley, rather a scrubby 18[mo], but the first edition after his death. I think Cowley has been Wordsworth's model in many of his lyrical rhythms and some of his curious felicities.

Cowley has often been called, in derision, *"the fantastic poet"*.

---

[1]) Mem. Introd., p. 78.

He must plead guilty to this charge as we have above remarked. He excelled in the mental gymnastics which characterize the poets called by Johnson "metaphysical".

This style is attributed by Johnson to an Italian, Marini, as its founder [1]). Marini died in 1625. His most important work was an Epic "Adonis". Guarini who died in 1612, the author of the celebrated "Il pastor fido", should also be named in this connection. The swollen and bombastic style of these writers had a decided influence on the German writers of the so-called "2nd Schlesien School" and also influenced the English poets of the 17th Century. We have preferred to refer this influence in Cowley to the euphuism of the 16th Century which may be traced to both Spanish and Italian influence. Johnson thinks John Donne (1631) was the introducer of the style into English *poetry*. Donne's versification was very harsh and tuneless. Southey says:

Nothing would have made Donne a poet unless as great a change had been wrought in the internal structure of his ears as was wrought in elongating those of Midas.

We have already spoken of this, happily defunct, style under head of Johnson's life of Cowley and there quoted from the Doctor's analysis of the same. Here are a few specimens from Cowley, as examples of this once popular style.

On Knowledge:

The sacred tree midst the fair orchard grew;
The Phenix Truth did on it rest,
And built his perfumed nest,
That right Porphyrian tree which did true logic show.

---

[1]) Johnson's Life of Cowley, p. 31.

Each leaf did learned notions give,
And the apples were demonstrative;
So clear their color and divine,
The very shade they cast did other lights outshine.

Envy to Lucifer, from the "Davideis":

Do thou but threat, loud storms shall make reply,
And thunder echo to the trembling sky.
Whilst raging seas swell to so bold a height,
As shall the fire's proud element affright.
Th' old drudging sun, from his long beaten way
Shall at thy voice start and misguide the day.
The jocund arts shall break their measur'd pace,
And stubborn poles change their allotted place.
Heaven's gilded troops shall flutter here and there,
Leaving their boasting songs tuned to a sphere.

Cowley says of Goliath:

His spear the trunk was of a lofty tree,
Which nature meant some tall ships mast should be.

Milton of Satan:

His spear, to equal which the tallest pine
Hewn on Norwegian hills, to be the mast
Of some great admiral, were but a wand,
He walk'd with.

It was probably such effusions as these to which
Dryden referred when he wrote the following of
Cowley: [1]

One of our late great poets is sunk in his reputation
because he could never forgive any conceit which came in
his way; but swept like a drag-net great and small. There
was plenty enough, but the dishes were ill sorted; whole
pyramids of sweetmeats for *boys* and *women,* but little of
solid meat for *men.* All this proceeded not from any want
of knowledge, but of judgment; neither did he want that in
discerning the beauties and faults of other poets; but only
indulged himself in the luxury of writing; and perhaps knew

---

[1] Dryden's Dedication of Juvenal, 1693.

it was a fault, but hoped the reader would not find it. For this reason a great poet, he is no longer esteemed a good writer: and for ten impressions which his works have had in so many successive years, yet at present a hundred books are scarcely purchased once a twelvemonth: for as my Lord Rochester said, though somewhat profanely, not being of God, he could not stand.

Such a superficial judgment could only arise from a superficial reading of Cowley:

Errors, like straws, upon the surface flow;
He who would seek for pearls must dive below.

Following out the figure of the drag-net which we may take, for a moment, to be the "glorius John" himself—would not the pearls—the solid matter, be likely to remain behind—waiting for those who dive below? Solid matter will assuredly be found, by all who seek, in Cowley's poems—and to his eternal honor be it said—solid matter which we now after the lapse of 200 years—gladly put into the hands of our *boys and women,* while a great portion of the "glorious John's" productions we as carefully guard from the same and consign to well deserved oblivion! Whether we ascribe it to the influence of Donne or to the prevailing taste, Cowley certainly disfigured many of his poems by this affected and to us distasteful style. It is always interesting but generally very difficult to trace the influences which have moulded a poet's mind or have given rise to his poetical creations. Poets are not often given to philosophising or to analysing themselves, and are not so ready to give an origin for their creations as the critics who come after, and "rush in where angels fear to tread". The subtle workings of the imagination—the transmuting power of fancy—

The light that never was on sea or land
The consecration and the poets dream.

6

Who will presume to trace and bring under rule and compass? "Who is sufficient for these things?" Lord Clarendon relates that Cowley always acknowledged his obligations to Jonson, but so close an observer as Dr Johnson could find wo trace of Jonson in his writings. The Pindarics might have been *suggested* by Jonson's Ode before mentioned, but a real *resemblance* cannot be traced. Edmund Gosse holds that the training and example of Dr *Henry More*, who was Cowley's contemporary at Cambridge, had a powerful influence on the Lyrics of Cowley. Dr More was founder and leader of the celebrated "Cambridge Platonists". His volume of Philosophical poems was published in 1640. Platonism had its last representative in More, he died in 1687. His writings are now little known. During his lifetime, however, they were very popular. "20 years together, after the Restoration, his works ruled all the booksellers in London."

"The Song of the Soul"—written in Spenserian stanza thus begins:

> Struck with the sense of God's good will
> The immortality of souls I sing:
> Praise with my quill Plato's philosophy.

Grosart thinks Spenser, even, is, in Cowley, "scarcely traceable from first to last". [1])

He also recalls only two traces of Shakespeare. The same critic says:

From the outset Cowley thought, imagined, felt for himself. An omnivorous yet cultured reader, he kept himself robustly independent on others. He assimilated rather than appropriated when from either classical or scriptural sources he drew inspiration and impulse.

---

[1]) Mem. Introd., p. 98.

Denham's words crystallize these thoughts into
poetry. [1])

> To him no author was unknown,
> But what he wrote was all his own.
> Horace his wit and Virgil's state
> He did not steal but emulate.

Another influence, than the euphuism which
we have been discussing, had an equally powerful
influence in giving outward form to Cowley's poetry.
English literature has always vibrated between two
influences—the rhetorical, didactic, classical, and the
untrained natural influence—modelled on no school
but "flowing at its own sweet will". The early part
of our century may be termed a period of decline
from that great Elizabethan age "when every branch
upon every tree rang with melodious voices". We
still hear the voics of Herrick, Drayton, Herbert—
the twilight melodies of that great and glorious
age—but "the noble though irregular music" was
dying away and only giving here and there faint
echoes of its former splendor.

What was to follow? What new influence was
now to act upon the English muse? Was it to be
from France, Italy, Spain? In each of these count-
ries the romantic poetry was undergoing a trans-
formation as in England. A decadence was per-
ceptible in all. At the end of the medieval period
had been a similar decline followed by the magni-
ficent outburst of the romantic. In what direction
would the next change lead? Anything more fervid,
spontaneous, fresh, could not be. The change must
be towards classical regularity. We may notice here
that the Scotch with whom we find so oft "the
native wood notes wild" predominating, had, singu-

---

[1]) Sir John Denham's Ode on Cowley's death.

larly enough, during the romantic period, cultivated a strictly classical style, influenced by their great classicist Buchanan. It proved to be in this direction that the new influence was to tend. The old heroic couplet of Chaucer was once more to take its place in our literature and rule there for 150 years, as the universal and popular measure. We shall, however, seek in vain for a further resemblance between the Chaucerian period and that which we are discussing. We listen in vain for the sweet pipings of another morn such as Chaucer heralded.

Old Chaucer like the morning star
To us discovers day from far.

sang Denham.

For such a day we must look far down the Centuries. The true Chaucerian revival—the revival of the rómantic narrative poem—came only in our own Century with the "Wizard of the north"—with the opening of that wonderful field of folklore of which the poets of the 17th Century were ignorant— of which Tieck sang:

Mondbeglänzte Zaubernacht,
Die den Sinn gefangen hält,
Wundervolle Märchenwelt,
Steig' auf in der alten Pracht.

Chaucer used the heroic measure with splendid success in the "Canterbury Tales". During the Elizabethan age it had been used in a loose degraded manner—being almost entirely lost in a free use of what the French call "enjambement"—in the words of Milton, "the sound being variously drawn out from one verse into another". Some of the best of the romantic poets had been able to give a charm to that which soon became weak in the hands of the less gifted. To this period of elegant variety and freedom succeeded the regular heroic rhymed couplet of five beats in each line, iambic pentameter. With the revival of the heroic couplet in the 17th Century four poets are identified in greater or less degree: Waller, Cowley, Denham and Davenant.

Waller.

Edmund Waller was the poet to whom the movement was due. His singular persistence in setting his face against the fashion of his age was remarkable in this Century which is ever cited as one pre-eminently conservative. More steadfast in literature than in politics was Waller—being one of those who could "wheel" at a short notice and accommodate himself to any party in power. Conscience never seemed to trouble him in the matter. This is the man who, according to Dryden,

first showed us to conclude the sense most commonly in distichs, which in the verse of those before him runs on for so many lines together that the reader's breath is lost in overtaking it.

Waller's life from 1605 to 1687 covers the period of the change of which we have spoken. In his youth the romantic was the popular style. Before he died, the precise and formal, the classical regularity of the rhymed couplet, was the universal measure of that which Gosse calls the "procession of the Commonplace".

Davenant.

Sir William Davenant, says Masson: [1]

had a remarkable inheritance of that language of light elevated, profuse and careless ideality which we recognize as the Elizabethan.

---

[1] Masson's "Life of Milton", vol. 6th, p. 277.

His principal work "Gondibert", an heroic poem, has much divided the critics. One of his friends has declared that the work is worthy to live as long as the "Eneid" or the "Iliad". This opinion called forth the following witty lines: [1]

Room for the best of poets heroic
If you "ll believe two wits and a stoic,
Down go the Iliads, down go the Eneidos;
All must give place to the *Gondibertidos*.

It is interesting to remember in connection with the name of this poet that it is possible we owe the life of John Milton to the good offices of Davenant. At the Restoration, when Milton's life was in danger, Davenant's influence kept his name off the list of those excluded from amnesty. We should add that Milton had, during the Protectorate, protected Davenant in like manner. [2]

Denham.

Sir John Denham was the first disciple of Waller. He used the couplet in his "Cooper's Hill". Four lines of this poem are so beautiful they should not be omitted "wherever and whenever" the poem is mentioned; of the Thames he says:

O could I flow like thee and make thy stream
My great example, as it is my theme;
Though deep, yet clear, though gentle yet not dull,
Strong without rage, without o'erflowing full.

It should also be remembered that this poem of "Cooper's Hill" is the first work in a department of literature which is now popular in our literature,

---

[1] Quoted from Morley's Sketches of Engl. Lit., p. 626.
[2] Collier's History of English Literature.

and which seems to be one which is confined to English literature almost entirely.

It may be called local or topographic poetry. The most illustrious disciple of this "new school" was our poet Cowley. A rather unruly one, however, as he was apt to wander off into new fields as fancy led. Dryden says of the trio Waller, Denham and Cowley:[1])

In all Greek or Latin non-dramatic poetry nothing so even, sweet and flowing, as Mr. Waller, nothing so majestic, so correct as Sir John Denham, nothing so elevated, so copious and full of spirit as Mr. Cowley.

So began the long reign of the heroic rhymed couplet which was to find, in the following Century, its most illustrious disciple in the "sage of Twickenham" and to be immortalized by being used as the measure of his translation of Homer.

One of the noblest monuments of our literature, notwithstanding Bentley's criticism:

it is a pretty poem, Mr. Pope, but you must not call it *Homer*.

Milton.

Through these years we have been following, another influence may have been working—we must ever remember that forming a background to this "court school of poets" was the majestic figure of Milton, emulating his own words "they also serve who only stand and wait". His early poems designated as Elizabethan archaisms—despised for his republican principles, but, soaring on the "seraph wings of ecstasy", in his darkened yet sublime old age. Accomplishing a work that in future ages was

---

[1]) Masson's "Life of Milton", vol. 6th, p. 380.

to overshadow all the rest of the 17th Century literature.

Wordsworth sang of him: [1])

Thy soul was like a star and dwelt apart,
Thou had'st a voice whose sound was like the *sea,*
Pure as the naked *heavens,* majestic, free.

As the "sea"—the "naked heavens" oft exert
an influence unseen, unfelt, so we cannot forbear
thinking, "the sweet echo" of "Comus", "Lycidas",
"L'Allegro", "Il Penseroso", was not without its
response in the poet soul of Cowley.

Though Waller introduced, the new style Cowley
was its most famous representative. His fame over-
topping that of the great master himself. "The greatest figure between Jonson and Dryden."

In his writings both styles are represented—on
the one side the romantic—on the other the solemn
didactic, and the classic regularity of the heroic
couplet. "The Silva", first appearing as en "addi-
tion to the second edition of the "Poetical Blossoms" (1636) contains a number of poems simple in
language with only here and there a trace of the
fantastic. The metres are various. Heroics mingled
with tetrameters.

"The Mistress" when it first appeared was claimed
by the new school but without good reason as there is
very little of the pure iambic pentameter in it. The style
in most of these poems is distinctly Elizabethan.
"Hope" and "Against Hope", two of the best, are
in mixed verse and several wholly in tetrameters.
"The Chronicle", one of the Miscellanies of 1656,
is wholly in tetrameters.

In the volume of "Occasional Verses", bearing
the date of 1663/68, we still find tetrameters though

---

[1]) Wordsworth's Sonnet on Milton.

the heroic verse predominates. In the "Davideis" and in a number of shorter poems he has given himself up completely to the influence of the new school.

Cowley stands with the small number of poets who have risen to great popularity during their lives. Who knew themselves to have won a niche in the temple of fame. This has been granted to few. Yet, as though fortune could not be too lavish of her gifts, he must be numbered with those whose fame has rapidly declined. Wood calls him the "prince of poets"—Clarendon represents him as "having taken flight beyond all who went before him"—Milton is said to have declared that the three greatest English poets were Spenser, Shakspeare and Cowley. And yet his name "has become a proverb for the instability of earthly fame".—The reasons for the popularity and the sudden fall, are not far to seek.

Cowley had sufficient of the gifts of genius—creative power—depth of thought—versatility—to have made him a great and popular poet in any age. While these contributed, they will not fully account for the almost unprecedented popularity during his life with a public which did not fully sympathize with his best efforts. There is a fashion in literature as in all else. The didactic, rhetorical poetry of Cowley suited the intellectual palate of a public cloyed with too much sweetness. Feeling, passion, the romantic, had been wrought up to the highest pitch of intensity and enjoyment. As in the physical, so in the mental a reaction is inevitable. Hence the popularity to which the intellectual element in Cowley's poetry lifted him. The polished regularity of the heroic couplet, the "cold elevation

and dry intelligence", even "Pindar's unnavigable
song" were adapted to produce a pleasing relaxa-
tion, a leading into new paths of the strained and
surfeited faculties.

Cowley's public, it should be remembered, was
the court, the aristocracy. Cowley was a court
poet. The taste of such a public is ever "variable
as the shade by the light quivering aspen made",
seeking, as the Athenians of old, something new.
To these causes may be ascribed the fame which
Cowley won during the 17th century with the court
public, with which he was closely identified.

Such a popularity has, of necessity, an element
of the factitious and ephemeral. A fall from such a
pinnacle of greatness is inevitable. But are the depths
to which Cowley has fallen so unfathomable?

Let his friend Grosart once more be heard:

Of Cowley I affirm, he has written things that all the
English speaking world over are (in Charles Lamb's prose)
'very dear' to choice spirits; he has made his mark on minds
that are potential on both the hither and thither side of the
Atlantic; he has added to the melody of our earth, so that
suppose his poetry and prose non-existent, golden and golde-
ning light would be absent and lyrical cries unuttered, he
has left wise, weighty, beautiful thoughts in finest English
words; he has, in short, added to the sum total of the rich
heritage that comes to men through books.

Let Cowley speak for himself his:

"Exegi monumentum ære perennius."

Begin the song and strike the living lyre;
Lo, how the years to come, a numerous and well-fitted choir,
    All hand in hand do decently advance,
And to my song with smooth and equal measures dance.
    Whilst the dance lasts, how long so'er it be,
My music's voice shall bear it company,
    Till all gentle notes be drowned
In the last trumpet's dreadful sound.

We claim that though the ephemeral, court popularity of Cowley has been swept away with the
pomp and vanity of the court itself—he had, and
ever has retained an enduring fame which no age
can obscure and bring under "ridicule and depreciation". A something which was not "for an age but
for all time".

Pope with his usual felicity strikes the right
chord:

> Who now reads Cowley? if he pleases yet,
> His moral pleases, not his pleasing wit,
> Forgot his Epic—nay Pindaric art,
> But still we love the language of his *heart*.

Yes, it is the language of the *heart* which

runs and as it runs forever will run on.

Works of Cowley.

Poetical Blossoms, 1633. Smallquarto 32 leaves.
  Second Edition, 1636; 3rd Edition, 1637.
Sylva, 1636.
Love's Riddle, 1638.
Naufragium Joculare, 1638.
Satire—Puritan and Papist, 1643.
The Mistress, 1647.
Cutter of Coleman Street, 1650.
Miscellanies, Folio, 1656.
Prose, 1661.
Latin Poems, 1668.

Authorities.

Sprat's Life of Cowley, 1668.
Johnson's Life of Cowley, 1780.
Cowley's Works, edited by Grosart, London, 1881,
  2 vol., 4°.
Lumby's Prose Works of Cowley, 1887.
Masson's Life of Milton, 1859—71.
Life and Works of Ben Jonson by Gifford.
Edmund Gosse, 17th Century Studies, London, 1885.
Ed. Gosse, History of 18th Literature, London, 1891.
Stebbing's "Cowley the Poet Politician."
Ward's History of Engl. Dram. Literature, London,
  1875.
A. Stern's "Milton's Leben", Leipzig, 1877—79.

INDEX.

CPSIA information can be obtained at www.ICGtesting.com
Printed in the USA
BVOW06s0557101115

426492BV00013B/131/P